Viking Attacks on Paris:

The *Bella parisiacae urbis*
of Abbo of Saint-Germain-des-Prés

DALLAS MEDIEVAL TEXTS AND TRANSLATIONS
7

Viking Attacks on Paris:

The *Bella parisiacae urbis* of Abbo of Saint-Germain-des-Prés

EDITION, TRANSLATION AND INTRODUCTION
BY

Nirmal Dass

(Toronto)

PEETERS
PARIS – LEUVEN – DUDLEY, MA
2007

Cover illustration: Victor Schnetz (1787-1870), *Count Odo defends Paris against the Normans in 885* (oil on fabric, 5.42 × 4.65 m). This painting was commissioned by King Louis-Philippe in 1834 for the Gallery of Battles at Versailles.
By kind permission of Réunion des Musées Nationaux / Art Resource, New York.

A CIP Record for this book is available from the Library of Congress.

© 2007 – Peeters – Bondgenotenlaan 153 – B-3000 Leuven – Belgium.
ISBN 978-90-429-1916-7
D. 2007/0602/58

Par animo quoque forma suo respondet.

Paris, *Bibliothèque nationale de France*, MS. lat. 13833, fol. 2r. This manuscript, which may well have been written by the hand of Abbo himself, is the sole witness to the complete text of the *Bella*.
By kind permission of the *Bibliothèque nationale de France*, Paris.

Editor's Foreword

The Dallas Medieval Texts and Translations series pursues an ambitious goal: to build a library of medieval Latin texts, with English translations, from the period roughly between 500 and 1500, that will represent the whole breadth and variety of medieval civilization. Thus, the series is open to all subjects and genres, ranging from poetry through philosophy, theology, and rhetoric to treatises on natural science. It will include, as well, medieval Latin versions of Arabic and Hebrew works. In the future, the publication of vernacular texts is a possibility. Placing these texts side by side, rather than dividing them in terms of the boundaries of contemporary academic disciplines, will, we hope, contribute to a better understanding of the complex coherence and interrelatedness of the many facets of medieval written culture.

In consultation with our distinguished board of editorial advisers, we have established principles that will guide the progress of the series. The primary purpose of the Dallas Medieval Texts and Translations is to render medieval Latin texts accessible in authoritative modern English translations; at the same time the series strives to provide reliable texts in Latin where such are not yet available. The translations are therefore established either on the basis of existing good critical editions (which we do not normally reprint) or, when necessary, on the basis of new editions. To enhance the accessibility of the texts to a wide academic public, including graduate students, the critical apparatus of the editions is limited to important variants. Each volume comprises scholarly introductions, notes, and annotated bibliographies.

Works published in the Dallas Medieval Texts and Translations are unexcerpted and unabridged. In the case of a work too long to appear in a single volume, we will start with the beginning of the work or publish integral parts of it, rather than creating a selection of discontinuous texts.

* * *

This seventh volume of our series offers an edition and translation of the *Bella parisiacae urbis*, an epic poem by Abbo of Saint-Germain-des-Prés which describes the Viking attacks on Paris in the ninth century. The *Bella* is a fascinating text at several levels. It is devoted to an important chapter of French history—so important, in fact, that King Louis-Philippe I commissioned a painting on its subject for the Gallery of Battles at Versailles. The painting, executed by Victor Schnetz, is reproduced on the cover of this volume. Moreover, Abbo's vivid depiction of the battles introduces the reader to the details of medieval warfare. His account makes for entertaining reading, yet leaves little doubt about the fact that medieval warfare was hardly less brutal than its technologically more advanced contemporary forms.

If the poem were made into a movie, it would receive an "R" rating for the violence it contains.

But Abbo did not intend the *Bella* to be an accurate historical account as we would understand the term. The poem views human history against the larger background of salvation. The battle between the Franks and the Vikings thus comes to be seen as a war between Christians and pagans, between the forces of God and those of darkness. Indeed, at the deepest level, such physical warfare is only an allegory for a battle that has to be fought within our souls: the battle between virtue and vice. This is why Book III of the *Bella*, which might, on the face of it, appear unrelated to the preceding two books, forms an integral part of the work as a whole.

Finally, the *Bella* is an intriguing literary composition. Its macaronic structure—that is to say, its frequent use of foreign Greek words, which interrupt the flow of the Latin text—emphasizes the tensions and the struggle that form the subject matter of the poem.

The author of this volume, Dr. Nirmal Dass of Toronto, is not only a fine scholar, whose learned introduction and notes explain the rich historical, theological, and literary dimensions of the *Bella parisiacae urbis*. What distinguishes his new translation from others is the fact that Dr. Dass is also a belletrist. Apart from numerous academic publications, he is the author of a successful novel, *City of Rains*.[1] Thus, in this English version of the *Bella* he has set out to wed scholarly precision with readability and, indeed, beauty. This aim accounts for the fact that his translation—especially that of the arcane Book III—is less literal and more literary than others. In his introduction, Dr. Dass strikingly writes: "the task of the translator is not only to be concerned with precision, but also symmetry—a translation redeems the source text, despite its sins." A translation must endeavor to transfer not only meaning from one cultural context to another, but beauty as well.

* * *

As usual, I conclude this foreword with thanks to the University of Dallas, whose financial support is making this series possible. Our publisher, Peeters of Louvain, deserves gratitude for taking on the series, and for producing it in such an attractive format. Finally, thanks are due to the medievalists in the United States and abroad who have agreed to serve on our board of editorial advisers or to assess individual manuscript submissions.

Philipp W. Rosemann
October, 2006

---

[1] Nirmal Dass, *City of Rains* (Saskatoon, Saskatchewan: Thistledown Press, 2003).

Table of Contents

Introduction

The Monk Abbo

The *Bella parisiacae urbis*, that is "The Battles of the City of Paris," is an epic poem written by Abbo, a rather obscure monk in the Parisian abbey of Saint-Germain-des-Prés. The poem dates from the late ninth century and describes two Vikings attacks in the years 885 and 886.

The little we know of Abbo is gleaned from his work, with scarce substantiating material from other sources. He tells us that he is a native of Neustria, present-day Normandy, and that he is a young monk and a deacon (*conlevita*) in the abbey of Saint-Germain-des-Prés, which once lay in the meadows along the left bank of the Seine; hence its name. He studied under Aimoin, a senior monk at the abbey, who had written a work describing the deeds and miracles of Saint Germain.[1] We are told that the teacher did not approve of the efforts of the pupil. Hereafter, there is not much else that we can state with certainty about Abbo the man, although three sources exist that perhaps shed light on his later years.

Firstly, a warden of the guesthouse of the abbey, named "Abbo," is mentioned in a charter dated February 25, 914 (or 919, depending on how the manuscript is to be read). Secondly, it is assumed that he died sometime after 922, since he published some of his sermons at the insistence of Bishop Fulrad of Paris, who held office from 921 to 927, and Bishop Frotar of Poitiers (ca. 900). Thirdly, there is a cryptic entry in the necrology of the abbey which states that an "Abbo" died on March 9. The year is not recorded.[2]

---

[1] Aimoin was a teacher at the monastery school of Saint-Germain-des-Prés, and flourished around 845; he likely died at the end of the century. Like his student, Aimoin also recounts details of two Viking attacks on Paris, in 857 and 858, under the chieftains Sigtrygg, Bjorn, and Hasting (Hastein). In the second attack, Abbot Louis of Saint-Denis was captured and held for ransom. See Carroll Gillmor, "Aimoin's *Miracula Sancti Germani* and the Viking Raids on Saint Denis and Saint-Germain-des-Prés," in *The Normans and Their Adversaries at War: Essays in Memory of C. Warren Hollister*, ed. Richard P. Abels (Woodbridge, England; Rochester, N.Y.: Boydell Press, 2002), 103–28; and Adelheid Krah, "Zeitgeschichtliche Aussagen in den *Miracula Sancti Germani* des Aimoin von Saint-Germain-des-Prés," in *Festschrift für Eduard Hlawitschka zum 65. Geburtstag*, ed. Karl Rudolf Schnith and Roland Pauler (Munich: Kallmünz, 1993), 111–31.

[2] See "Necrologium S. Germani," in *Les obituaires de la province de Sens*, vol. I, 1, ed. Auguste Molinier (Paris: Receuil des historiens de la France, Obituaires, 1902), 253. Abbo's sermons, which also were influential, especially in Anglo-Saxon England, remain unedited. They are found in a manuscript at the *Bibliothèque nationale de France* (MS. lat. 13023).

The Manuscript

The unique witness of the entire *Bella* is found in the *Bibliothèque nationale de France,* MS. lat. 13833, which might well have been written by the hand of Abbo himself, since this manuscript remained in the abbey, where Abbo had left it, for nearly 700 years. Only in the sixteenth century is it found, and that briefly, in the collection of Pierre Pithou.[3]

The manuscript consists of 43 parchment folios, in quarto, with eighteen lines per page, and it dates from the late ninth century. There are several glosses and annotations to be seen, which are likely the work of Pithou, and which have not been included in this edition, since they are not integral to the original. Their value lies in deriving a readable translation, and certainly they have been used to that end. The purpose of this edition is to provide a fresh reading of the sole manuscript that contains the entire poem, with certain emendations and alternative readings.

The Problem of Book III

The first two books, which deal with the Viking attacks on Paris, were little known in their day. But the third book received a wide circulation, so that twelve versions of it exist as distinct manuscripts.[4] The appeal of Book III, in the years that followed Abbo's writing of it, stemmed from its purposeful use of arcane words, both Latin and Greek, which delighted the learned men of that time. Thus, curiously, Abbo accrued fame not for his rather stirring and often rigorous narrative of the defense of Paris by that city's inhabitants, nor for his skill, at times a little deficient, with dactylic hexameters (the presence of Virgil does indeed loom large throughout the *Bella*). Rather, he acquired renown because men (and they were invariably men) turned to Book III when they sought an exotic word or two. Thus, Book III entirely eclipsed the other two books.

An inverse bias took hold among latter-day scholars who held Books I and II to be historically instructive, while they neglected Book III, deeming it to be of little literary worth; even merely an afterthought to the real business at hand—the Viking attacks. We need to

---

[3] Pierre Pithou (1539–1596), the renowned jurist and scholar, was an ardent collector of manuscripts. After his death his entire collection went to the royal library in Paris, which later became the *Bibliothèque nationale de France.* See Louis de Rosanbo, "Pierre Pithou. Biographie," *Revue du XVIᵉ siècle* 15 (1928): 278–305.

[4] The number of manuscripts extant for Book III is, in fact, thirteen, if we include the complete version (with all three books) in the *Bibliothèque nationale.* The various manuscripts are listed in Anthony Adams and A. G. Rigg, "A Verse Translation of Abbo of St. Germain's *Bella parisiacae urbis*" (see Annotated Bibliography), 3, n. 6. See also Patrizia Lendinara, *Anglo-Saxon Glosses and Glossaries* (Aldershot, England; Brookfield, Vt.: Ashgate, 1999), 157–98.

reconsider this stance, since it is the result of a skewed approach to Abbo's poem. There is great value in reading the entire three books of the *Bella* as a seamless and organic whole. Book III makes sense only within the context of the first two books; and the entire poem becomes a rather polished literary endeavor when we measure it in its entirety.[5]

Date of Composition

It is difficult to be precise as to when Abbo finished his poem, but it is probable that he did so within ten years of the events that he relates. Internal evidence tells us that the entire epic spans a period of eleven years, from November 24, 885, to the autumn of 896. And, although he refers to Odo as king (who was crowned on February 29, 888), he does not mention Odo's death, which occurred on New Year's Day of 898. This leads to the assumption that Abbo had completed his poem by 897.

The Macaronic Structure of the Bella

The entire poem consists of 1,393 lines, that is, 660 lines in the first book, 618 in the second, and 115 in the third. Throughout, Abbo has striven to maintain the dactylic hexameter, despite frequent slippage; it was a meter, as he likely well knew, that was most apt for writing an epic.

As noted already, in the past, a rather damaging view has prevailed according to which the first two books are to be seen as a unity, while Book III is nothing more than Abbo's clumsy, and therefore spurious, attempt at mirroring the Trinity, and is consequently of little use.[6] This extreme stance serves only to highlight critical blindness and should not be considered a viable hermeneutical tool.[7] The *Bella* is concerned not with historical accuracy—such a view will always undermine the poem's agenda—but with theology.

---

[5] On the knowledge of Greek in the Carolingian age, see Walter Berschin, *Griechisch-lateinisches Mittelalter. Von Hieronimus zu Nikolaus von Kues* (Bern and Munich: Francke Verlag, 1980), and *The Sacred Nectar of the Greeks: The Study of Greek in the West in the Early Middle Ages*, ed. Michael W. Herren and Shirley Ann Brown (London: King's College, 1988).

[6] This view is represented by Henri Waquet, *Abbon. Le siège de Paris par les Normands* (see Annotated Bibliography), vii. In his edition, the entire third book is excised.

[7] "Hermeneutical" does not refer to the viewpoint advocated by Michael Lapidge in his article, "The Hermeneutic Style in Tenth-Century Anglo-Saxon Literature," *Anglo-Saxon England* 4 (1975): 67–111. For Lapidge, "hermeneutic style" designates the employment of Greek and glossed words in a given text. For our purposes, hermeneutics is both symbolic communication and the move to uncover the ontological conditions that give rise to symbols.

We can never know whether Abbo wished to impose upon his poem a tripartite structure in imitation of the Trinity, since intent has long vanished with the author, and there is little to be gained in trying to guess what it might have been. But the residue of his endeavor remains—and it is this residue that we must examine.

The structure of the *Bella* is properly to be defined as macaronic, in that it is written in a mixture of Latin and Greek.[8] This practice is discernible in the entire poem, but is most prevalent in Book III. But why does Abbo use this device? Aside from the desire of a young man to "show off" perhaps, the macaronic elements, which may better be described as code-switching, serve three very distinct purposes. Firstly, they are emphatic; they heighten language. Secondly, they provide solutions to metrical difficulties and lend rhetorical elegance. And thirdly, they are used in moralistic summaries. Let us briefly examine these functions.

(1) In Book II, line 164, we read, *Francorum Karolo supra-fato basileo*, that is, "To the emperor of France, Charles, mentioned above." Abbo uses the Greek term *basileus* for "emperor." He does not use the corresponding Latin one (*imperator*). Just as English tends to use French terminology to lend a quality of *savoir-faire*, or Latinate and Greek terminology when scientific rigor is required, so Abbo uses *basileus* to heighten the political importance of Charles and set him apart from the various other titled men of the poem, such as counts, bishops, and Viking "kings." By using Greek, Abbo purposefully places an impediment in the flow of the Latin, a linguistic roadblock that forces us to pay attention to the language that describes the special nature of Charles's power, and to stress the fact that the French are governed not by heathen kings, as are the Vikings, but by an emperor whose claim to power descends, through the hallowed conduit of Rome, from God Himself.[9]

(2) In Book III, line 40 reads, *Declina birotum, bravium capito ac cliotedrum*: "Turn aside the two-wheeled chariot; take up the prize and the ecclesiastical seat." Here, the meter requires a word with fewer syllables than those in the Latin equivalent (*sedes episcopalis*). Thus, Abbo turns to the hybrid word *cliotedrum*, which is a collapsed form of the Greek *klinokathēdrion*, a recliner. As well, *cliotedrum* offers a more elegant solution to the metrical demands over the more clumsy and overly technical Latin phrase *sedes episcopalis*.

---

[8] See M. M. Bakhtin, *The Dialogic Imagination*, ed. Michael Holquist, trans. Caryl Emerson and Michael Holquist (Austin: University of Texas Press, 1981), 263, 289, 411ff.

[9] It is important to note that neither Charlemagne nor any of his descendents were called "Holy Roman Emperors." This term did not come into use until the mid-thirteenth century when it described the kingdom established by Otto I in particular. Charlemagne and Charles the Fat took the title of *Occidentalis Imperator*, or "Emperor of the West"—that is, Emperor of the Western Roman Empire—as opposed to the Emperor of the East (*Orientalis Imperator*)—that is, the Eastern Roman Empire, ruled from Constantinople.

(3) In Book I, lines 114–15 state, *P geminum fidos, raro quamvis, vegetabat, M que truces posthac chile seranta chile id extat*: "He gathered twice P of the faithful, how few, while the cruel ones were a thousand times forty, or forty thousand." Abbo uses Greek numerals (*P* for 100, *M* for 40, and *chile* for 1000) to make a moralistic summary— Christians will triumph over the barbaric pagans; ungodly forces cannot defeat them. The overwhelming odds also underscore the play of miracles, which pervade the narrative and allow for the transformation of impossibility into possibility, of impending defeat into victory.

However, these three facets of the macaronic elements in the poem are not independent—rather they are interdependent; all three facets and functions are set into motion whenever Abbo mixes Latin with Greek. The macaronic in the *Bella* is continuously emphatic, metrically elegant, and a summary of the moral outlook of the entire poem.

Moreover, within these macaronic elements both dialogue and polyphony coexist, wherein contending opposites create tensions, transitory unions, and furtive discourses. Thus, the poem is also about disruption, such as the barbarity of the Vikings, and the moral laxness of the Franks (outlined in Book III, namely, vanity, sexual confusion and promiscuity, and religious negligence, all of which destroy the soul). Abbo's text employs the many arcane words as viable tools to embed a dialogic discourse—for each poem is always a dialogue with many meanings, other texts, with readers, and with structures of power (the economic devastation, the political uncertainty, the fragile nature of civilization). The *Bella* as a macaronic text engages in dialogue with different readers (us, Aimoin, the monk Gozlin, God, Saints Mary, Germain and Geneviève), with the idea of empowerment (kings versus God and the saints, civilization against chaos, legality touching illegality, rebellion against authority, the swearing of false oaths), and with the literary past (Virgil, the Bible, classical learning). Each time we encounter an arcane word in the *Bella*, we are forced to ask questions, to seek out meanings, to wander in the universe that surrounds each and every utterance.

The dialectic of the macaronic structure in the *Bella* is discernible in each part of the whole, *pars pro toto*, in such a way that each component reflects the whole in a metonymic process. Thus, for example, line 38 in Book III reads: *Nam scrupulum generant ΨΙΧΗ vexantque pupillas*: "They will blight not only your eyes but also blemish your soul." The Greek term *psychē* immediately disrupts the flow of the Latin, being an entirely alien word, and is even written in a little understood script (Greek). However, this disruption brings into play a theological discourse, since *psychē* means "soul," which must be kept pure that it might properly find its eternal home, where only purity can exist. In this one word is contained the entire agenda of the *Bella*, that is, salvation.

The Historical Context

The poem spans an eleven-year period, as noted, from 885 to 896. These were tumul-
tuous and eventful years. They saw the establishment of a "Danelaw" in France, namely,
in Normandy; the demise of the Carolingian line; and the beginnings of the Capetian
dynasty, which would eventually rule France until 1789.

These events cluster around the lives of men with which the *Bella* fully acquaints
us—King Charles the Fat, Count Odo of Paris, Emperor Arnulf and his son Swentibold, and of course the Vikings, or the Danes, or Norsemen, as the *Bella* prefers to call
them.

The poem mentions others, of course; mostly churchmen and members of the
nobility, such as the Bishops Gozlin and Anscheric, Count Heinrich, and Abbot Ebolus. Two heavenly beings complete the cast. They are Saints Geneviève and Germain.
In the hexameters of the poem, these characters play out their deeds against a back-
drop of uncertainty, strife, sorrow, and then triumph. And there are many side-char-
acters who otherwise would have remained unknown: men such as the twins Segebert and Segevert, the warriors Gerbold, Sclademar, Erilang, Gozwin, Einhard,
Hardrad, Arnold, Eriveus, and Odoacer. These warriors have achieved renown through
the efforts of Abbo, his monument of words—their heroic deeds endure, and their
names are remembered. In Frankish and Germanic tradition, leaving behind fame was
akin to immortality. These individual warriors have achieved what they would have
valued the most.

When the Vikings attacked in 885, Paris was not a particularly important city in the
kingdom of West Francia, but it was an easy target, lying as it did along the banks of
the Seine River, whose waters the ships of the Danes plied without great difficulty.
Vikings prowling on the rivers of France was not unusual, for the days of a strong Frankish hegemony had died with Charlemagne in 814. His descendents proved weak and
ineffectual, defects evidenced in the reign of his great-grandson, Charles the Fat
(832–888).

Nearly one year before the attack, in December of 884, it had seemed that Frankish
supremacy might again be realized in the person of Charles. In that year, he inherited
the kingdom of the West Franks from his brother, Carloman, who died without heirs.
Earlier, he had come into possession of the realm of his other brother, Louis the Younger,
and was crowned king of Italy and emperor of the West Franks in 879 and 881, respec-
tively. The vast empire of Charlemagne seemed again to be united under Charles, who
now held sway over Germany, Lotharingia, France, Italy, Burgundy, and Provence. But
he was not Charlemagne and could not control internecine strife. His nephew Arnulf,
the illegitimate son of Carloman, rebelled, seeking the kingdom of his father, and in 887
succeeded in wresting Germany away from Charles; he was crowned king of the East

Franks in November of that year. Charles did nothing and instead chose to retire to his palace at Neidingen, where he died within two months, on January 13, 888.[10]

The reign of Charles had also seen greater and bolder raids by the Vikings into West Frankish territory, or present-day France. Instead of fighting them, Charles paid them off with ransom, or tribute (what we might term "protection money"). This strategy only bought short-term peace, since the Vikings returned each spring to collect; and because Charles had no system of defense, these raiders chose to winter in France rather than return to their homes in Scandinavia or England, to save the inevitable return trip.[11] Thus, permanent Viking armed camps were established in areas of western France. One such armed camp would eventually lead to the creation of Normandy, or the land of the Norsemen, under Charles the Simple, the eventual successor to Charles the Fat.

A policy of appeasement and payment meant that cities such as Paris were left to fend for themselves—as well as cities like Boin, Fécamp, Rouen, Nantes, Cordoue, Redon, Meaux, and Chartres, each of which eventually fell to the Norsemen.[12]

Given that the territories ruled by Carolingian kings were immense, they often appointed governors, or *missi dominici*, for each region, and a count or duke for each important city. These men were overeers on behalf of an absentee king. Paris also had such an official—Count Odo, who resided permanently in the royal palace on the Île-de-la-Cité, and who was known as the Count of Paris and the Duke of France.[13]

Odo (ca. 860–898), who was the son of Robert the Strong (d. 866),[14] came to prominence because of the events related in the *Bella*; events which also undermined the authority of King Charles the Fat. The *Bella* minutely relates what occurred when the Vikings struck at Paris, on November 24, 885. The Danes wanted Paris because of its two bridges that spanned both currents of the Seine to the north and south of the Île-de-la-Cité; these bridges thwarted ready access to the rich regions of the Marne and

---

[10] See Simon Maclean, *Kingship and Politics in the Later Ninth Century: Charles the Fat and the End of the Carolingian Empire* (New York: Cambridge University Press, 2003).

[11] See Einar Joranson, *The Danegeld in France* (cited in the Annotated Bibliography), and Simon Coupland, "The Frankish Tribute Payments to the Vikings and their Consequences," *Francia* 26:1 (1999): 57–75.

[12] The subject of Viking incursions into France is widely examined, but see in particular Judith Jesch, "Vikings on the European Continent in the Late Viking Age." Useful also are Jean Renaud's *Les Vikings en France* and the same author's *Les Vikings et la Normandie*. (These titles are cited in the Annotated Bibliography).

[13] Details on the life and reign of Odo may be found in Édouard Favre, *Eudes, comte de Paris et roi de France, 882–898* (see the Annotated Bibliography).

[14] Robert the Strong, who died in 866, was the Count of Angers and Tours, regions that he held as a *missus dominicus*, or provincial governor, for King Charles the Bald (823–877), against whom he rebelled, winning for himself the dukedom of the land between the Seine and Loire. Like his son Odo, Robert also actively fought the Vikings and was killed in a battle against them at Brissarthe, near Châteauneuf-sur-Sarthe. The Capetian rulers of France were his descendents.

Burgundy. The Grand Pont linked the north bank of the Seine and was a stone structure, with two defensive towers on either end. The south bank was linked by a wooden bridge (the Petit Pont), which was also protected by towers, although wooden ones.[15]

Paris did not fall to the Vikings, despite their ferocity, for Odo and Bishop Gozlin ably defended it.[16] In time, Charles the Fat responded to the pleas for help by the Parisians and appeared at the head of a large army. But instead of fighting the Danes, he chose to negotiate with them and came to an agreement according to which he would pay them off with 700 pounds of silver and allow them unhindered passage into Burgundy. For their part, the Norsemen agreed to abandon all plans to capture Paris, though they would eventually attack it again.

This agreement did not sit well with the Parisians; it was the free passage up the Seine that irked them the most. Thus, they refused access, forcing the Danes to portage their ships past the two bridges and float them again upstream. These events brought into focus Odo's strength and Charles's weakness. Soon thereafter, in 887, Charles was deposed, just as the eastern portions of his realm rose up in rebellion, led by his nephew Arnulf.[17]

On February 29, 888, Odo was elected king of the West Franks by the Frankish nobility; great was the need for a strong man to defend the realm ably against the Vikings, whose threats and attacks had in no way abated—the payment of ransom only shifted their incursions elsewhere. The necessity of a vigorous ruler meant that the royal, Carolingian heir, Charles the Simple, was overlooked because of his youth. In time, his

---

[15] When the Vikings attacked, it is probable that the inhabitants of Paris found refuge in the Île-de-la-Cité, which had stout defensive walls; in its Western section stood the royal palace, in which Odo lived. In the Eastern part was found the Church of Saint-Étienne, to which were joined the Basilica of Notre-Dame and the Baptistery of Saint-Jean-le-Rond; these three ecclesiastical buildings were under the direct rule of Bishop Gozlin. Charles the Bald had previously fortified the two bridges that connected the Île-de-la-Cité. The Grand Pont on the right bank was aligned with rue Saint-Denis and by 861 was protected by a fortified tower (later known as *le grand châtelet*). The smaller bridge on the left bank, the Petit Pont, was also fortified with a tower (later called *le petit châtelet*). The tower that the Vikings attack in the *Bella* is the one protecting the Grand Pont; the tower of the Petit Pont was never attacked. See Colin Jones, *Paris: A Biography of a City* (London: Allen Lane, 2004), 1–36.

[16] Bishop Gozlin is the first "fighting bishop" to appear in medieval literature. His other famous counterparts include Bishop Jerome in *The Cid*, and of course Bishop Turpin in *The Song of Roland*. He has historical parallels as well, such as Bishop Odo, the half-brother of William the Conqueror, whose exploits at the Battle of Hastings are fully displayed in the Bayeux Tapestry. There is also a later example from the fourteenth century, Bishop Henry Dispenser.

[17] Arnulf (850–899) was the illegitimate son of Carloman of Bavaria (Charles the Fat's older brother). Arnulf was given the March of Carinthia as his demesne but was forbidden to inherit the kingdom of his father because of his birth; hence his rebellion against his uncle, Charles the Fat, who was also the King of the East Franks. For various aspects of the life and reign of Arnulf, see *Kaiser Arnolf: Das ostfränkische Reich am Ende des 9. Jahrhunderts*, ed. Franz Fuchs and Peter Schmid (Munich: Beck, 2002).

claims would become a constant irritant to Odo, who would have to fight to retain his crown—a situation made even more precarious by the fact that the Emperor Arnulf, who originally supported Odo, now took up the cause of his nephew, Charles the Simple.[18] This led to an extended civil war, which the *Bella* hints at, until Odo was forced to cede some territory to Charles and recognize him as his heir. As for the Vikings, they continued their harrying. Indeed, despite having defeated them resoundingly at Montfaucon in the Argonne (mentioned by the *Bella*), Odo was also eventually forced to pay them tribute to buy peace, just as Charles the Fat had done. Odo died on New Year's Day of 898. Charles the Simple succeeded him.[19]

Aside from the human characters, the *Bella* also introduces two celestial ones: Saints Geneviève and Germain. This intermingling of the heavenly and the mundane transforms the *Bella* into a work of magical realism, where the ordinary becomes fully charged with the otherworldly and earthly events take on symbolic import. In this respect, of course, Abbo draws upon St. Augustine's notion of progressive history, in which God has an active hand.

Saint Germain (496–576) was the bishop of Paris and a faithful subject of the Merovingian king, Childebert, whom he encouraged to abandon worldly pleasures in favor of piety, and whom he persuaded to destroy pagan practices in Gaul, which had managed to persist. Germain was widely known for his generosity of spirit and his ardor in alms-giving. In the civil war that followed the death of Childebert, fomented by the royal princes, Germain worked tirelessly for peace, but he died before he could see stability return to the land. He was buried in the Church of Saint Vincent in Paris. During the reign of Pepin the Short, the father of Charlemagne, Germain's bones were reinterred, and the Church of Saint Vincent was renamed Saint-Germain-des-Prés, that is, Saint-Germain-of-the-Meadows, since it was located in the fields along the left bank of the Seine. Even in his lifetime, Germain was much revered for his piety and his godly

---

[18] Charles the Simple (879–929) would play the most important role in the history of France—he would create the French Danelaw, or the province of Normandy, where Danes had heavily settled and whence they could not be routed. It was the best course of action for Charles, by way of which he neutralized much of the Viking threat to the heartland of France. For details on Charles the Simple and his rule, see Auguste Eckel, *Charles le Simple* (cited in the Annotated Bibliography). For his treaty with the Vikings at the ford of Saint-Clair-sur-Epte and the creation of Normandy, see Eleanor Searle, *Predatory Kinship and the Creation of Norman Power, 840–1066* (cited in the Annotated Bibliography), 40–7.

[19] In one sense, Charles the Simple's "feud" continued with Odo, even after the latter's death. In 922, the nobles proclaimed Robert I (865–923), the brother of Odo, as king; he is mentioned in the *Bella* as "Rotbert." Charles the Simple moved to suppress this claim and at the Battle of Soissons in 923, Robert was killed. The nobles immediately elected Duke Rudolf of Burgundy (d. ca. 936), who proved the stronger, and who imprisoned Charles to become king of the West Franks. Charles died a prisoner in 929. His son, however, Louis d'Outremer, would eventually come to power. But the future belonged to the descendents of Robert, whose grandson, Hugh Capet (938–996), became the progenitor of the Capetian line.

influence on King Childebert; in the *Bella* he takes on the role of a fighting-saint and becomes the poem's true hero, because he is consistent in his love for the city and its inhabitants, and his actions are not determined by the dictates of expediency, as are those of kings (both Charles the Fat and even Odo).[20]

Saint Geneviève is the very first patron saint of Paris. Legend has it that she was a peasant girl from Nanterre, born around 420, who was instructed in piety by Saint Germain. It is said that she moved to Paris with her godmother, named Lutetia (the Gallo-Roman name for the city), where she lived for the next thirty years, and where she devoted herself entirely to works of charity and extreme piety. Legend has it that in 451, Attila, the leader of the Huns, spared Paris from being sacked because of the prayers of Geneviève. She died in 512 and was buried in the Church of Saints Peter and Paul, which was renamed in her honor.[21]

It is around these four protagonists, two contemporary and two celestial, but especially Saint Germain, that the *Bella* structures its narrative, in which even the Vikings seem only literary props that allow Germain to manifest his great powers.

The Theology of the Bella

The *Bella* is a poem about heroic action, which serves two ends: the repelling of the Vikings raiders, and the salvation of the soul. For Abbo, the two struggles are one and the same. Both these ends come together in one hero: Saint Germain. Germain's influence, even in death, is shown to be strong; Paris is part of his demesne, and therefore he is a more able protector of the city and its people than are the secular rulers. When King Charles, and ultimately Odo, fail to drive back the Vikings, Germain descends from heaven to contend with the heathen enemy himself, and his actions prove far more effective than those of any other leader or warrior in the poem. The saint is the hand of God made visible in history.

The *Bella*, consequently, is an epic poem about conflict—spiritual, moral, political, and physical. This structure is expressed by way of agonistic dualities: internal goodness (exemplified by the city of Paris, the sanctity of churches, Frankish society, the very geography of France, and the redeemed soul), versus the external evil (represented by

---

[20] See Dom Jacques Bouillart, *Histoire de l'abbaye royale de Saint Germain des Prez* (Paris: G. Dupuis, 1724). Gregory of Tours also mentions one of the miracles of Saint Germain; see his *History of the Franks*, trans. Lewis Thorpe (Harmondsworth: Penguin, 1977), 466.

[21] For the life of Saint Geneviève and her cult, see Moshe Sluhovsky, *Patroness of Paris: Rituals of Devotion in Early Modern France* (Leiden: Brill, 1998), and Dom Jacques Dubois and Laure Beaumont-Maillet, *Sainte Geneviève de Paris: la vie, le culte, l'art* (Paris: Beauchesne, 1982).

destruction, desecration, the Vikings, conflict, chaos, disorder, and the damnation of the unredeemed soul). This structure is further associated with the conflict between forces that are Satanic (the Vikings) and those that are godly (the saints). But both can manifest themselves only within the bounds of geography in its various manifestations; that is, the land of France and the individual body. The Vikings ravage the former, while sin ruins the latter. The Norsemen, or Danes, are thus also the embodiment of sin and the ruination it can bring.

This duality, however, is resolved not simply by the defeat of the Other (the pagan Vikings), because there is also contention within—France is being ravaged by the Vikings for a reason: her body is diseased by sin, while her rulers are weak and negligent, not caring for the flock that God has put in their trust. Just as a body sapped of its strength falls prey to illness, so France because of its sin (excessive opulence, greed, pride, and lust, both natural and unnatural) is a land enfeebled, which has invited the calamities that now beset her in the form of the rapacious Danes. This sin extends further to the Frankish rulers, who have forgotten to be true and faithful Christian kings. The body politic is riven by fractious rebellion and the expediency of self-interest. The rulers of France have fallen into sin; they have abandoned their royal duty, for the piety of kings is protection of the land and people.

When the *Bella* describes the Vikings surging toward the walls of Paris, their ships ranged upon the current of the Seine, we are not reading a photographic description of what is occurring. Instead, we have before us a melee of interconnected signs that must be decoded and understood. All action is filled with such signs in the *Bella*, and these actions in turn are interwoven with words (signs), all of which together must be read as the alphabet of the divine, through which alone can God "speak"—that is, make His purpose known, and by the aid of which His will is to be read and obeyed. In this way, the *Bella* becomes *historia*, the semiosis of history as theology, of deeds and acts as allegory. Both heaven and earth enter into an intertextual relationship—the one struggling to survive despite the onslaught of sin, and the other eternally continuing, despite the disruption of Satanic forces, and providing the ever expansive context of salvation.

This theological turn in the text, marked by the first appearance of Saint Germain (Book I, lines 471ff.), also highlights the salvific process—the preservation of the city (Paris), wherein the Christian citizens (the Franks) live, and which is ruled by a divinely anointed king. This earthly hierarchy reflects the City of God, ruled by the perfect, heavenly King, where the elect and the redeemed abide. Actions in the *Bella* continually mirror the progress of humanity toward salvation, thus translating Abbo's observations into interpretative acts.

Therefore, the *Bella* chronicles the various events of the attacks and the ensuing siege because they are also manifestations of God's plan for humanity. The strife and pain of battle are similar to the struggle against sin and evil. Without a divine plan, suffering is merely nameless and unnamable cruelty, in that it holds no meaning. The medieval mind searches for divine meaning hidden in all things; the task of the *Bella* is the revelation of this meaning to those who cannot see beyond the blood and the anguish brought on by the Danish marauders. Thus, the Vikings are a great wash of heathens (sin) assaulting the Christian body (Paris and France), which must defend itself by physical and spiritual means—by donning both physical weapons and the complete armor of God. It is theology that allows for the construction of meaning amidst the senselessness of fierce battle.

By the end of the second book, the revelation of God's plan is complete, and the discourse becomes that of repentance—the abandonment of pleasures, wealth, and greed. It is within the context of penance and atonement that the many heroic individual acts are to be read, such as those of Ebolus, Gerboldus, Ragenar, Segebert, Segevert, and the various other Frankish warriors. Next, repentance is contrasted with the impenitence of the rulers: King Charles the Fat chooses to buy off the Vikings rather than fight them; Count Odo, though once valiant, loses his moral authority when he becomes king and follows the same neglect as his predecessor. The discourse of royal power, which displays itself as monolithic, is destroyed when it is juxtaposed with the divine imperative to redeem.

Given that the *Bella* is concerned with a salvific agenda, there is a tendency toward exaggeration. The concern of history in the medieval world was not to preserve a meticulous record of actuality (which is ultimately impossible), nor was there any interest in writing down a full explanation as to how and why an event occurred, simply for the sake of constructing a record. The medieval mind was steeped in teleology, and intellectual endeavor sought to find meaning between action and divine will. To search for strict accuracy in the works written in the Middle Ages is ultimately futile, for in them action can acquire meaning only when it is lifted into the higher or greater context of theology.

Without the salvific imperative, the defense of Paris bears no significance and is perhaps not worth undertaking—a point of view embodied by Charles the Fat when he chooses to buy off the Vikings rather than fight them. Charles neglects not only his duty as a Christian king, but he also thwarts the workings of divine intercession. Paying the Vikings becomes cynical expediency, for it accepts that God is powerless to stop evil. Charles's policy of appeasement further denies the fulfillment of God's plan of redemption, since it temporarily lulls the contention of good and evil, thereby hindering the revelation of the metaphysical within the metaphorical.   Given the discourse of salvation, the *Bella* aptly possesses a threefold structure, which mirrors the triune nature of God. This is a sophisticated move, through which the text becomes the literal manifestation of God's redemptive nature: the mortal flesh becomes redeemed in the Word, and the body finds completion in the eternal discourse of parenthood and progeny in the Father, Son, and Holy Spirit.

The *Bella* also becomes a melding of both gesture (the actual and heroic defense of Paris) and discourse (the narrative of this event, the display of arcane words in the Latin text, physical and spiritual geography). Both gesture and discourse are fully elaborated in the first two books. The middle ground between gesture (deed) and discourse (word) may properly be named as translation (salvation), wherein the body is changed into the soul and is lifted into heaven, or that perfected place where the need for both acts and speech ends. In other words, Abbo proceeds to draw a moral summary of both deed and discourse, which he has elaborated at length in the first two books, by turning to explanation (translation, bearing across meaning) in the third book. Why does God allow suffering to afflict His people? The answer is embodied in the final book of the *Bella*.

Book III, then, is not an afterthought, or an awkward attempt at achieving theological symmetry. Rather, all three books are seamlessly bound one to another in a grand process embedded in the processes of the internal and the external. Whereas the first two books deal with events outside the body, the third book delves inside the body and uncovers the assaults on the soul and how they are to be repulsed. In the third book, the duality of the internal and external finds its fullest expression, which binds the first two books within the salvific schema that is continually being enacted in the mundane world. The third book, therefore, is an allegory of the Holy Ghost, the third member of the Trinity, who translates both the word and the deed into modes of salvation.

Edition and Translation

There have been several editions of the *Bella* in the past, and the one presented here differs from these in that it re-examines the unique witness in the *Bibliothèque nationale de France* (MS. lat. 13833) and presents variant readings and emendations.[22]

Although this translation cannot claim to be the first one into English of the entire three books of the *Bella*, it may be seen as being the most accessible. Previous translations are either not in English, incomplete, or suffer from excessive literalism—a shortcoming that ultimately defeats the purpose of a translation: readability. The translation undertaken here adheres closely to the intended meter of the source text, the dactylic hexameter; "intended" because the original shows slippage and unevenness. The shortcomings of the original are not followed, for the task of the translator is not only to be concerned with precision, but also symmetry—a translation redeems the source text, despite its sins.

---

[22] For the previous editions of the *Bella*, see the Annotated Bibliography below. I would like to extend my sincerest thanks to the staff of the *Bibliothèque nationale de France* for their kindness and generosity in offering me the greatest assistance in my endeavors.

A few words about translating Book III, which presents a most unique challenge, would be appropriate at this point. The discourse of the third book depends on the proverb, or gnomic verse, wherein meaning is collapsed and sentiment adumbrated. This results in a source text that is vague at best, since the proverbs presented have entirely lost their context, namely, the society for which they were apt. Consequently, the translation of Book III has involved a process whereby meaning has had to be provided, since a literal rendering of the proverb cannot properly be housed in the target text (English). Within each proverb a precarious balance has to be struck between sense and nonsense, in order for meaning to be constructed. The duty of the translator, therefore, becomes that of supplying what is lacking—a useful and usable context—without which we veer into nonsense, where all syntactical and logical unity breaks down, and we are left with a series of words strung together that hold little or no significance outside of grammatical correctness. Our target text, this translation, consequently fills in the consistent lack inherent in Book III in order that the balance of the proverb may be rightly and harmoniously maintained.

Annotated Bibliography

Primary Sources

Although various early editions of Abbo's *Bella* appeared from about the mid-sixteenth century onward into the eighteenth century, these editions are of little use today, aside from the questions of reception. A standard edition was not established until Paul von Winterfeld's *Abbonis Bella parisiacae urbis*, Monumenta Germaniae Historica, Poeatae Latini aevi Carolini 4/1 (Berlin: Weidmann, 1899; reprinted, 2000). This edition is both a rigorous study of the source material and a thorough correction of the various errors that were prevalent in the edition published earlier by Georg Heinrich Pertz, *Abbonis de bello Parisiaco libri III*, MGH Scriptores rerum Germanicarum in usum scholarum separatim editi 2 (Hanover: Hahn, 1871).

Translations

Given the intriguing and thrilling subject matter of the first two books of the *Bella*, it is not surprising that these have been consistently translated, while the third book has been neglected. However, the *Bella* had never been translated in its entirety into Englsh (or any other language) until most recently by Anthony Adams and A. G. Rigg, "A Verse Translation of Abbo of St. Germain's *Bella parisiacae urbis*," *The Journal of Medieval Latin* 14 (2004), 1–68. This translation is good for the many useful footnotes that help elucidate the often difficult text, and for the fact that it is a good crib to the Latin. Most useful also is the French translation of the first two books, in prose, by Henri Waquet, *Abbon. Le siège de Paris par les Normands* (Paris: Les Belles Lettres, 1964), which is a reprint of an earlier (1942) edition. Although this is a dual text, Waquet's Latin follows Winterfeld very closely. There is also the valuable French translation (again only of the first two books and again in prose) by Johannes Steenstrup, *Les invasions normandes en France* (Paris: Albin Michel, 1969), 232–82. A German translation of just the first book was done by Anton Pauels, *Abbo von Saint-Germain-des-Prés, Bella parisiacae urbis, Buch I* (Franfurt: Lang, 1984), in which the critical apparatus is most useful and the prose translation very readable.

Critical Approaches to the Bella

The critical attention that Abbo's poem has received in the past may be divided into two types: that which is concerned with the first two books and that which examines only the third book. In fact, aside from introductions to editions, the *Bella* has never been examined as a literary text; it is only regarded as a curious and minor historical document, and nothing more. Thus, we have general historical studies about the Viking incursions into France that use the *Bella*, such as Jean Renaud's *Les Vikings et la Normandie* (Rennes: Éditions Ouest-France, 1989), and Jean Petitjean, "Abbon l'humble: son poème sur le siège de Paris par les Normands," *Annales de la faculté de Caen* 4 (1988): 61–74. The studies concerned with the language of Book III are certainly more in number, the best among them being by Patrizia Lendinara, "The Third Book of the *Bella parisiacae urbis* by Abbo of Saint-Germain-des-Prés and its Old English Gloss," which is part of her larger study of glosses in Anglo-Saxon England, namely, *Anglo-Saxon Glosses and Glossaries* (Aldershot, England; Brookfield, Vt.: Ashgate, 1999), 157–75. However, there is precious little critical study of the *Bella* as a whole, that is, one which encompasses not only its historical importance, its linguistics peculiarities, and its reception in the early Middle Ages, but which also closely analyzes its intricate and often elegant literary merit.

History of the Period

Abbo wrote during a turbulent period, when the ailing Frankish polity was crumbling under the relentless attacks of the Vikings, and a new system of self-government, regionally-based, was emerging. Count Odo (or Eudes in French) precisely embodied this new order, and thus he has the distinction of being the first king of France, and indeed the first Capetian. The old biography of this fascinating and powerful leader by Édouard Favre remains the best, namely, *Eudes, comte de Paris et roi de France, 882–898* (1893; reprinted, Geneva: Slatkine, 1976). Works dealing with Charles the Fat and Charles the Simple are many, but those worthy of use are Simon Maclean, *Kingship and Politics in the Later Ninth Century: Charles the Fat and the End of the Carolingian Empire* (New York: Cambridge University Press, 2003), and the old work by Auguste Eckel, *Charles le Simple* (1899; reprinted, Geneva: Slatkine, 1977). Both books are especially helpful in providing a historical context to the *Bella*. Books that deal with Charles the Simple tend to emphasize his handling of the Norman crisis and the creation of Normandy, which was the direct result of attacks such as the ones described in the *Bella*. However, Rosamond McKitterick's *The Frankish Kingdoms under the Carolingians, 751–987* (London and New York: Longman, 1983), succeeds in maintaining a broader focus on the eventual demise of the Carolingian dynasty, a theme which the *Bella*, unwittingly, addresses.

The Vikings

The success of the Norse raiders in France depended not so much on their innate martial prowess, but rather on the systemic weaknesses of the Carolingian rulers: the lack of centralized command, the inability to raise a permanent defense force, and the ready willingness to buy off the Vikings. To gain an overview of the effects of the Norse incursions into France Jean Renaud's *Les Vikings en France* (Rennes: Éditions Ouest-France, 2000) is very helpful. As to how successfully the Vikings established themselves in northwestern France, Eleanor Searle's *Predatory Kinship and the Creation of Norman Power, 840–1066* (Berkeley: University of California Press, 1988) is especially useful. Although dated, Einar Joranson's *The Danegeld in France* (Rock Island, Ill.: Augustine Library Publications, 1923) is a sound exploration of the concept of Viking settlements in France, to which Charles the Simple had little choice but to agree. In the same vein, Judith Jesch's "Vikings on the European Continent in the Late Viking Age," in *Scandinavia and Europe, 800–1350*, ed. Jonathan Adams and Katherine Holman (Turnhout: Brepols, 2004), 255–68, serves to underscore the fact that the Norse were seeking far more than plunder; they were intent on settlement, which they effectively achieved from Ireland to Russia.

Abbonis *Bella parisiacae urbis*

Viking Attacks on Paris:
A Translation of Abbo's
Bella parisiacae urbis

Table of Sigla

A = MS. Paris, *Bibliothèque nationale*, lat. 13833
GP = *Abbonis de Bello parisiaco libri III*, ed. Georg Heinrich Pertz
PW = *Abbonis Bella parisiacae urbis*, ed. Paul von Winterfeld
HW = *Abbon. Le siège de Paris par les Normands*, ed. Henri Waquet

SCEDULA SINGULARIS CERNUI ABBONIS DILECTO FRATRI GOZLINO

Cunctorum Dei plasmatum extimus et conlevita indignus Abbo, sincaere omnemque terrigenam superantis igne dilectionis amplexando fratri Gozlino, quicquid in Christo utriusque vitae manet iocunditatis. Tuae admodum mihimet acceptissimae germanitatis affectio sibimet dudum destinari crebro poposcit, ut bellorum Parisiacae polis, praecellentissimi quoque principis ab examine regni hucusque Odonis, nostro genitum labore codicellum didicit, tam contigui studiosa ingenioli quam fraterni insuper non inmemor flagri. Eandem itaque ob gratiam faustissime noveris germane, tibi hancce dirigi pagellam, cum tam rara ne umquam penes me frustretur petitio, tum solamine omnium apud lectorem amicissimi, ut cara finetenus vice illam mittentis fungatur, quin etiam a deviis prudenti dextera relevetur. Numquam enim otio reficiendi ob scolarum pluralitatem, cuius commoditati ubique locorum vacaverim; verum qui primum fuerit prolata, constat adhuc sequens pagina membranis semel tantum mutatis, post quoque ceu quopiam Foebo tuo sagaci lustretur arbitrio.

Denique, huius aeliminata directionis causa, aequum autumatur depromi geminas etiam opusculi inchoationis. Quarum siquidem prima fuerit causa exercitacionis (tunc etenim adhuc litteratoriae tyrunculus disciplinae Maronis proscindebam aeglogas), altera vero mansuri aliarum tutoribus urbium exempli. Caeterum tam tuae quam reliquorum quidem lectorum almae caritati non istud metricae conplecti volumen, quod vates taxer, notum fore molior. Nullatenus quippe hic, quae penes summos repperiuntur figmenta poaetas. Atqui Faunos ferasve nusquam tripudio carminis in ludum more Sileni conglomeraverim neu rigidas motare cacumina quercus coaegerim; tum vero silvae avesque, menia quoque numquam nostris sunt comitata vestigiis prae dulcedine cantionis; nec quovis modulamine Orco aliisve Manibus animas tartarea aeripuerim caligine ritu Orphei. Plane etiam si quando affuerit velle, nusquam tamen his actibus favit posse. Ergo nec positor quidem nuncupor nec figmenta hic habentur; sed nostrae facultatis adsint presidia.

A LETTER OF DEDICATION BY ABBO, THE MOST HUMBLE, TO HIS BELOVED BROTHER GOZLIN

Abbo, the least of God's creatures, unworthy deacon, embraces his brother Gozlin,[1] with an affection that is pure, sincere, and higher than any found on earth, and wishes for him, in Christ, all the happiness that we are able to obtain both in this life and the next.[2] Your brotherly love, most dear to me, has impelled me, time and again, to dedicate to you this little work, devoted to the battles of Paris and to Odo, the most notable prince, the foremost of all the leaders of men that this kingdom has produced down to the present day; this little work, as you well know, is born of our labor, and greatly testifies to your deep interest in my most meager talent, and demonstrates that you have not forgotten our brotherly love. Know then, O happiest of brothers, that a similar emotion urged me to address to you these simple pages, not only to ensure that so precious a love may not be disappointed on my account, but also to satisfy the very best friend among readers, so that these pages may fulfill to the very end the precious task for which they are being sent forth, and above all that your wise hand may clear up the imperfections found in them. Indeed, being preoccupied with my studies, to which I have devoted myself entirely, I have not found the leisure necessary to revise these pages.[3] Thus, they are presented to you for the first time, such pages as now follow; only the parchment has changed. Skim through them with your wise judgment, like another Apollo.[4]

Having laid bare the purpose of this narration, it is good, I think, to make known the two reasons for which I decided to undertake this little work. The first was to embark on a literary exercise (for I was but a simple student of letters and had read the *Eclogues* of Virgil for the first time).[5] The second was my intention of leaving behind an enduring example to those who are guardians over other cities.[6] As for the rest, I leave it to your benevolent love, and to that of other readers. Know that though I have undertaken to write this volume of verse, it is not meant to make me into a poet. Here you will see none of those fabrications often found in the work of grand poets. Indeed, nowhere have I gathered Fauns and wild animals dancing, singing, or frolicking, after the example of Silenus.[7] Nowhere have I forced rigid oak trees to rustle their tops. For the sake of charm, my song shall have neither forests, nor birds, nor even high walls, to keep company with my meters. None of my verses shall follow the example of Orpheus and seek to snatch away from Orcus, or from other infernal deities, the souls of those plunged into the darkness of Tartarus.[8] It is perfectly obvious that I have never had such a desire, nor do I have the ability to accomplish such an undertaking. Therefore, I do not take on the name of poet, and these are not fictions that I present.[9] Rather, I have used the means available to me to complete my task.

Porro triadi nostros credidi biblos visu et auditu modo decusatos. Quorum duo quidem tam praeliis Parisiacae urbis, Odonis quoque regis, quam profecto almi ac heroys praesertim mei Germani eiusdem sedis olim egregii praesulis, effulgent miraculis, alias tamen quibuslibet inauditis. Qui autem supplet trinitatem tercius, horumce ignarus constat. Nam cleronomos, tametsi angustum maneat situm, decentissime ornat: tum scolasticis ambientibus glosas suis in commentis obnixe complacet, allegoria vero aliquantisper, cui eius indago libuerit, renitet; tum per semet quoniam mutis inhaeret verbis, propria manu linguas superieci.

Pedes autem in omnibus opusculi versibus adeo delegerim, quo per rarissimos forte ignorantia potiusve oblivione liquerim clodos; qui tamen periergia quaeso industriaque legentis debitae virtuti restituantur. Pentimimeris nempe seu cum cata triton trocheon eptimimeris rata similitudine per omnia currunt cesurae, quanquam bucolice ptomen per pauca. Communibus praeterea bannitae modis cum dieresi et aepisinaliffa non dense usus extiti. Igitur largiente divino munere suggessit haecine mihi facultas. Quid plura? Catalecticus cunctus existit versus. Tum multa prorsus alia lectori seria parebunt indita. Nec tamen putetur hoc ob aliud factum, nisi materiam vel a tua, dulcissime frater, prudentia hauriendam seu cuiuspiam alterius diserti, cum ad manus venerit, metrici. Dactilici quidem versiculi trimetri praepositi causam enucleant sui; sed minime exauditi. Verum, quod haud apud magistrum, saltem mereantur nancisci penes germanum.

Gaudia quot radii Febo, tibi sint et honores,
Cum fine in finem, clam quoque fine Deo.

EXPLICIT EPISTOLA.

I have divided these books into three, which are ornamented solely by those things that I saw and heard. Two of these books are notable for their account of the battles fought around Paris and those fought by King Odo, and also for the miracles, otherwise unknown, performed during the siege by my dear and most benevolent master Germain, who was once the bishop, without equal, of this city.[10] As for the third book, which completes the trinity, it is manifestly different from the story of the siege. Therefore, it takes up very little room, and it seeks to provide clerics with methods of effective literary adornment. It will be suitable for students who search for terms for their compositions. Allegory will also very briefly shine forth for those who admire such things. But, because allegory often works by way of obscure words, I have written the glosses on top with my own hand.[11]

As well, for all the verses of my work, I may have chosen meters that grow clumsy, caused perhaps by my ignorance but more likely by my forgetfulness, but at least they will be few in number. And I pray the careful and industrious reader to bring these verses back to their true quality. The caesuras are penthemimeral, or with a trochee in the third foot, hepthemimeral, and they are consistent throughout, except for the rare occasions when the Bucolic caesura is used.[12] Further, I have seldom made use of elision or dieresis or episynaloephe, which lie beyond common poetic usage.[13] Here, then, is presented, by the grace of God, that for which I have had the skill. What more is there left to say? All the verses are catalectic. The reader will find sown in the work various other things. However, do not think that this work has had any other purpose than to offer material by way of which your learning, O my dearest brother, may be drawn forth—your learning, or that of some other person versed in meter, if my book were to come into his hands. And it is with that confidence that some dactylic trimeters reveal their reason for being used, though they may not be properly heard. While the teacher may not judge these verses to be worthy, they may at least find favor with a brother.

May your joys and honors be many as the rays of Phoebus;
And may you come to find your end with God, who is without end.

HERE ENDS THE LETTER.

VERSICULI AD MAGISTRUM DACTILICI

O pedagoge sacer meritis
Aymoine piis radians
Digneque sidereo decore:
Perrogitat mathites liniens
Ore pedes digitosque tuos,
Cernuus Abbo tuus iugiter.
Sume botros, tibi quos tua fert
Vitis adhuc virides; rubeant
Imbre tuo radiisque tuis.
Continuo seris atque fodis   10
Tu, celebrande, putas et eam.
Nuncque cupis nitea pluviis
Alterius, iubare alterius.
Dulce cui tribuas rogo mel.
Nam tibi palmes et uva manet.
Floruit has mihi Parisius
Nobilis urbs, veneranda nimis,
Bella precans sua ferre tibi.
Agnita cuius ut orbe vago
Sepiat aethera palma volans,   20
Doxaque regent ubique micans,
Ore tuo gradiente super.

A LITTLE DACTYLIC VERSE FOR MY MASTER

Aimoin, O splendid master, bright with worth[13]
And goodness, worthy of heavenly light,
Your student, the humble Abbo begs you
With entreaties, as he yet ceaselessly
Kisses your mouth, your feet and your fingers,
That you consent to receive these grapes,
The harvest from your vine, though they be green.
The rain and the sunshine that you will send
Over them, will make them red with ripeness.
Without respite, you sow and also dig,   10
O worthy teacher, then you prune your vine,
That it might grow in the rain and the sunshine.
Bestow on it, I pray, your sweet honey:
This vine and these clusters belong to you,
And they flowered for me in this noble
City of Paris, which is most famous;
And of its battles I beg to tell you,
So that its victory may be made known,
And fly up and resound in the heavens,
So that the air may become filled with it,   20
And may its glory, increased by your mouth,
Hold sway and be resplendent over all.

INCIPIT LIBER PRIMUS
BELLORUM PARISIACAE URBIS.

Dic alacris salvata Deo, Lutecia, summo.
Sic dudum vocitata, geris modo nomen ab urbe
Isia, Danaum latae media regionis,
Quae portu fulget cunctis venerabiliori;
Hanc Argiva sitis celebrat peravara gazarum.
Quod nothum species metaplasmi modo nomen
O collega tibi Lutecia pingit honeste,
Nomine Parisiusque novo taxaris ab orbe,
Isiae quasi par merito pollet tibi consors.

Nam medio Sequanae recubans, culti quoque regni   10
Francigenum, temet statuis per celsa canendo,
"Sum polis, ut regina micans omnes super urbes."
Quae statione nites cunctis venerabiliori.
Quisque cupiscit opes Francorum, te veneratur.
Insula te gaudet, fluvius sua fert tibi giro
Brachia complexo muros mulcentia circum.
Dextra tui pontes habitant tentoria limfae
Levaque claudentes; horum hinc inde tutrices
Cis urbem speculare falas citra quoque flumen.

Dic igitur, praepulchra polis, quod Danea munus   20
Libavit tibimet soboles Plutonis amica,
Tempore quo praesul Domini et dulcissimus heros
Gozlinus temet pastorque benignus alebat?
"Haec," inquit, "miror, narrare potest aliquisne?
"Nonne tuis idem vidisti oculis? Refer ergo."
Vidi equidem iussisque tuis parebo libenter
Haec tibi nempe litaverunt libamina saevi:
Septies aerias centum praeter iuniores
Quamplures numero naves numerante carentes   30
Extat eas moris vulgo barcas resonare.
Quis adeo fartus Sequanae gurges fuit altus
Usque duas modicumque super leugas fugiendo,
Ut mirareris, fluvius cui se daret antro

HERE BEGINS THE FIRST BOOK OF
THE BATTLES OF THE CITY OF PARIS.

In the year 885.
Shout with joy, Lutetia, you who were saved by God on high.[14]
This is how you were known in days long ago, but now you take
Your name from Isia city that sat on the Danaan plain,[15]
Whose harbor shone forth as the brightest embellishment of all;
That same Isia for whose treasures the greedy Argives yearned.[16]
A bastard name, indeed, a sort of metaplasm for you,
Isia's rival, but which describes you well, O Lutetia.[17]
It is by this new name, that is Paris, that the world knows you;
This means you are Isia's twin; no difference between you both.

Now, in the region of Sequanus is found the rich kingdom[18]   10
Of the Franks. Raise yourself up high, now, so that you may sing forth:
"I am that city, dazzling like a queen over all cities."
And you too are renowned for your harbor, much praised by others.
Those that covet the wealth of the Franks come to pay you homage.
An island rejoices in you, and a river stretches out[19]
Around you in a perfect embrace that caresses your walls.
To your right, to your left, on your banks are bridges that hold back
The waves. Here and there are towers that guard the bridges;
Some of these face the city; others face out to the river.

Speak, most wondrous of cities, of the gift the Danes brought for you,   20
Those friends of Pluto, in the time when Gozlin, the Lord's bishop,[20]
The sweetest of heroes, the mildest of shepherds, governed you.
"Astonished am I," she said, "that no one has spoken of this.
Did you not see with your own eyes what came to pass? Speak of that."[21]
Indeed, I saw everything, and gladly I obey your will.
Now, here are the gifts the cruel ones brought to offer you:
Seven hundred high-prowed ships and very many smaller ones,
Along with an enormous multitude of smaller vessels
The very ones that in the vulgar tongue are often called barques.[22]   30
The deep waters of Sequanus were so overly crowded,
For a distance that extended more than two leagues downriver,
That one asked in amazement, Where had the river vanished?
It could not be seen, hidden, as though by a veil of fir, oak,

Nil parens, abies quoniam velaverat illum
Ac quercus ulmique simul, madidae sed et alni
Urbem quo tetigere quidem Titane secundo,
Egregii Sigefredus adit pastoris ad aulam.
Solo rex verbo, sociis tamen imperitabat.
Vertice flexo ad pontificem sic inchoat ore: 40
"O Gozline, tibi gregibusque tuis miserere;
Ne pereas, nostris faveas dictis, rogitamus.
Indulge siquidem, tantum transire quaeamus
Hanc urbem. Tangemus eam numquam, sed honores
Conservare tuos conemur, Odonis et omnes.
Hic consul venerabatur, rex atque futurus.
Urbis erat tutor, regni venturus et altor."

Haec contra domini praesul fidissima iecit:
"Urbs mandata fuit Karolo nobis basileo,
Imperio cuius regitur totus prope kosmus
Post Dominum, regem dominatoremque potentum,   50
Excidium per eam regnum non quod paciatur,
Sed quod salvetur per eam sedeatque serenum.
Ut nobis si forte tibi commissa fuissent
Menia quodque peregisses iustum tibi narras
Quid fore sancires?" Sigemfredus: "Caput," infit,
"Ensis honore meum, canibus demum quoque dignum.
Toxica, ni tamen his precibus caedas, tibi tela
Nostra ministrabunt castella die veniente,
Decedente famis pestem, hoc peragentque quotannis."
Haec ait atque dehinc abiit, sociosque coegit.   60

Sic caput Aurora rapuit perdente duellum.
Nempe ruunt omnes ratibus turri properantes,
Quam feriunt fundis acriter complentque sagittis.
Urbs resonat, cives trepidant, pontesque vacillant;
Concurrunt omnes turrique iuvamen adaugent.
Hic comites Odo fraterque suus radiabant
Rotbertus, pariterque comes Ragenarius; illic
Pontificisque nepos Ebolus, fortissimus abba.
Hic modicum praesul iaculo palpatus acuto,
Hic eius iuvenis miles simili Fredericus   70

Elm, and alder, each one entirely drenched by the water.
And when in two days these ships made landfall hard by the city,
Siegfried did make his way to the great hall of the famed shepherd;
Though king in name only, he still commanded many warriors.[23]
After bowing his head, he addressed the bishop in these words:
"O Gozlin, show mercy to yourself and the flock given you.   40
That you may come not to ruin, grant our plea, we ask you.
Give us your consent that we might go our way, well beyond
This city. Nothing in it shall we then touch, but shall preserve
And safeguard all the honors that belong to you and Odo,
Who is the noblest of all counts and who is the future king.
Guardian of this city, he shall become the kingdom's rampart."[24]

Then the Lord's bishop, in greatest loyalty, offered these words:
"By our king, Charles, have we been given this city to guard;
By him, whose majestic realm spreads almost over the whole earth,
By the Lord's will, and who is King and Master of the mighty.   50
The realm must not suffer by the destruction of this city;
But rather this city must save the realm and preserve the peace.
Now, if by chance, these walls were entrusted to you, as they are
To us, and you were asked to do all that you have asked of us,
Would you deem it right and agree?" Siegfried said: "By my honor,
Rather my head were lopped off by a sword and thrown to the dogs.
However, if you do not agree to my requests, we shall
Have our siege engines, at daybreak, hurl poisoned darts at you;
With sunset you shall know hunger's curse. It shall go on for years."[25]
Thus having spoken, he went his way and assembled his men.   60

Now, when dawn had nearly faded away, the battle began.
Jumping into their boats, the Danes headed for the tower,
And began to hurl stones at it and riddled it with arrows.
The city grew noisy; people grew fearful. Bridges swayed.
Everyone rushed about, trying to help defend the tower.
It was then that Count Odo did shine, along with his brother
Rotbert, as well as Count Ragenar. Then it was also that
Ebolus, stalwart abbot, the bishop's nephew, proved worthy.[26]
At that place, the prelate was hit by a sharp-pointed arrow,
And at the same place, a young warrior, Frederick, was struck down[27]   70

Est ictus gladio; miles periit, seniorque
Convaluit, sese medicante Dei medicina.
Hic vitae multis extrema dedere, sed acres
Pluribus infigunt plagas, tandemque recedunt,
Exanimes Danos secum multos referentes.
Iam occidui medium vergebat ad ultima Tile
Climatis australis quoque Apollo secutus Olimpho.

Nil prorsus species turris renitens erat adhuc
Perfectae, fundamentis tantum bene structis
Ac modicum ductis sursum factisque fenestris   80
Gaudebat; belli sed eadem nocte peracti
Altius haec circumductis crevit tabulatis;
Lignea sescuplae siquidem superadditur arci.
Sol igitur Danique simul turrim resalutant;
Praelia devotis iaciunt inmania valde;
Pila volant hinc inde, caditque per aera sanguis,
Conmiscentur eis fundae laceraeque balistae;
Nil terras interque polos aliud volitabat.
At turris nocturna gemit dardis terebrata.
Nox fuit eius enim genitrix, cecini quoque supra.   90
Urbs pavitat, cives strepitant, et classica clamant
Absque mora tremulae cunctos succurrere turri.
Christicolae pugnant belloque resistere curant.
Belligeros inter cunctos gemini radiabant
Plus aliis fortes, alter comes, alter et abba;
Alter Odo victor, bellis invictus ab ullis,
Confortando fatigatis vires revocabat,
Lustrabat iugiter speculam perimens inimicos.
Qui vero cupiunt murum succidere musclis,
Addit eis oleum ceramque picemque ministrans,   100
Mixta simul liquefacta foco ferventia valde,
Quae Danis cervice comas uruntque trahuntque,
Occiduunt autem quosdam quosdamque suadent
Amnis adire vada. Hoc una nostri resonabant:
"Ambusti Sequanae ad pelagos concurrite, vobis
Quo reparent alias reddendo iubas mage comptas."
Fortis Odo innumeros tutudit. Sed quis fuit alter?
Alter Ebolus huic socius fuit aequiperansque

By a sword. The young warrior died, but the old man recovered,
Thanks to divine medicine, administered to him by God.[28]
For many there, this was the last moment of their lives;
But others dealt out bitter wounds, and forced the Danes to fall back,
Who carried away with them many of their lifeless friends.
By now, Apollo, and all of Olympus, had veered westwards,
Soon sinking between ultimate Thule and the southern regions.[29]

Now the tower did not shine forth with all its magnificence,
For it was far from finished. But its foundations were solid
And stood firmly grounded. Proudly it rose; its crenels were sound.[30]   80
During the night that followed, after the battle had ended,
A wooden tier was built all the way around the tower,
Raised atop the old bastion, and half as high as before.
Thus, together, the sun and the Danes beheld this new tower.
The latter were soon locked in a frightful fight with the faithful.
Arrows flew here, there through the air; blood gushed and flowed;
Darts, stones, and javelins were hurled by ballistae and slingshots.[31]
Nothing was seen, between heaven and earth, but these projectiles.
The many arrows made the tower, built in the night, groan out;
It was the night that gave it birth, as I have chanted above.   90
Fear seized the city—people screamed, battle horns resounded
Calling everyone to come and protect the trembling tower.
Christians fought and ran about, trying to resist the assault.
Among all the warriors, there were two most outstanding
For their valor: one was a count, the other an abbot.
Victorious Odo was one, never routed in battle;
He fortified those who were exhausted; revived their strength,
And rushed about on the tower, striking down the enemy.
As for those who sought to dig beneath the walls with iron picks,
He served them up with oil and wax and pitch, which was all mixed up   100
Together and made into a hot liquid on a furnace,
Which burned the hair of the Danes; made their skulls split open.
Indeed, many of them died, and the others went and sought out
The river. And then our men, with one voice, loudly exclaimed:
"Right badly scorched are you! Run now quickly to the Sequanus.
Its current will allay your pain and restore your flowing manes."[32]
Dauntless Odo struck down many. But what of the other one?
This other was Ebolus, his companion and his equal—

Septenos una potuit terebrare sagitta,
Quos ludens alios iussit praebere quoquinae.   110
Hisce prior mediusve fuit circumve nec ullus;
Fortiter ast alii spreta nece belligerabant.
Verum stilla quid est simplex ad caumata mille?

P geminum fidos, raro quamvis, vegetabat,
*M*que truces posthac chile—seranta chile id extat—
Hice recenter eunt vicibus turrim, iuge foedi
Ingeminant bellum. Clamor fremitusque fit altus,
Ingentesque replent voces hinc inde ruentes
Aethera; saxa fremunt parmas quatientia pictas,
Scuta gemunt, galeae strident traiecta sagittis.   120
Huc praeda redeunt equites, certamina stipant,
Incolumes adeunt speculam saturique ciborum,
Anteque durcones multi repetunt morientes,
Quam lapides iaciant illamque gravent lapidando.
Dulce quibus flamen Danae spirantibus aiunt,
Quaeque suo lacerans crines lacrimansque marito:
"Unde venis? Fornace fugis? Scio, nate diabli,
Hanc nullus poterit vestri superare triumphus?
Non tibi nunc Cererem vel apros Bacchumque litavi?
Tamque cito quare repedas ad tegmina stratus?   130
Haec iterum gestisne tibi poni? Redeuntne,
Elluo, sic alii? Similem mereantur honorem."
Clibanus ob humile quantum speculae sinuatus
Saeva per ora duit quamvis ignobile nomen.
Ima dehinc ardent eius disscindere sciri.[1]
En inmane foramen hians, maius quoque dictu.
Apparent penitus proceres iam nomine citi,
Cristatosque vident cunctos, quibus atque videntur,
Conspiciuntque viritim omnes non introeuntes.
Horror enim vetuit quod non audacia sumpsit.   140
Orbita mox a turre teres iaculatur in illos,
Bis ternis arcens animas direxit Averno,
Perque pedes tracti numerum complent morientum.

---

[1] GP and HW give scisci, while PW provides fusci. A may be emended to sciri.

With a single spear, he pierced seven Danes all at once,
And in jest he said to his own to take them to the kitchen.[33]   110
In battle none outshone, equaled, or compared with these two men.
However, many did fight most courageously and scorned death.
But indeed what is a single drop for a thousand fires?

Among the faithful were no more than two hundred warriors;
The grim ones were a thousand times forty, or forty thousand;[34]
They sent fresh troops dashing to the tower. O most horrid sight!
They only fought fiercely. A great, quaking clamor arose;
It could be heard on both sides—a mighty chorus of voices
Filled the air, as hurtling rocks thudded into painted shields.
These shields let forth groans and helmets clattered as swift arrows fell.   120
Some horsemen, returning from their pillaging, rode forward
To join the fight at the tower—well-rested and fed were they.
But many among them got no chance to hurtle their stones,
For they were struck down and killed; the rest ran back to their ships.
Before drawing their last anguished breath, the dying Danes tore
At their hair and shed tears. Then their wives cried out:
"So, you have run back from that furnace! I know, you Devil's son!
But not even one among you shall chance upon victory.
Was it all for nothing I gave you Ceres, Bacchus, boar meat?[35]
Why are you so quickly exhausted that you seek out shelter?   130
Were you hoping to have a second meal? Glutton! Is this why
The others return, too? A fine welcome they will also get!"[36]
These rude mouths drove them to make their own domed furnace near
The bottom of the tower, whose very name they greatly scorned.
The hard Danes ardently sought to breach the tower's foundations;
An immense breach appeared—wide-gaping beyond description.
As was readily seen, there appeared, at the bottom,
Those gallant warriors, whose names have already been mentioned,
With helms on their heads. They and the Danes beheld each other,
But the Danes held back, gripped by an insurmountable horror.   140
Suddenly, a huge wheel was thrown from the top of the tower
Right upon the Danes, laying low six, whose souls were sent to Hell;
They were dragged off by their feet and joined the throngs of the dead.

Tum foribus posuere larem, Vulcania cura,
Hinc multare viros rentes et perdere turrim.
Fit rogus horribilis, fumusque teterrimus inde
Nubila militibus miscet, succedit et umbris
Scilicet arcs piceis, hora veluti diuturna.
Nam tulit haec minime sufferre diu sibi notos,
Sed nostri Dominus miserescens vertere iussit   150
In sortem caecam populi nebulam generantis.
Fortius ille furens Mavors regnare sategit.
Signifer en geminus concurrit ab urbe benigna,
Lancea bina gerens, speculam conscendit, amictum
Auribus inmodicis croceum, formido Danorum.
Tunc centena quium pepulit cum sanguine vitam
Centeno catapulta nimis de corpore pernix,
Hospiciumque comas ducti lintresque revisunt.
Lemnius hic moritur claudus, magno superante
Neptuno; humectant latices incendia fusi.   160
Pestiferae gentis miles percussus acerbo
Rotbertus felix iaculo spiravit ibidem,
Atque Deo pauci vulgo periere iuvante.
Erubuere tamen posthac veluti lupus audax
Nil rapiens praedae, repetitque quidem nemus altum,
Subtilemque nimis secum retulere fugellam,
Tercentum exanimos flentes Charone receptos.
Nox comitans turris studuit vulnus medicari.
Haec duo bella sui residens in limite currus
Ante November adest gelidus supplere Decembri   170
Solibus is caudam ternis quam caederet anni.

Sole suos fulvo radios fundente sub aethre
Sorte Dionisii lustrant equidem recubantes
Macharii Sequanae ripas, et castra beatum
Germanum circa teretem componere vallis
Commixto lapidum cumulo glebisque laborant.
Post montes et agros, saltus, camposque patentes
Ac villas equites peragrant peditesque cruenti.
Infantes, pueros, iuvenes canamque senectam,
Atque patres natosque necant necnon genetrices.   180
Coniugis ante oculos caedem tribuere marito,

Then they set the gate alight with fire guarded by Vulcan,
By which they hoped to burn our men and destroy the tower.
A dreadful pyre formed and smoke billowed up in ghastly clouds
That enveloped the warriors. And then, within an hour,
The fortress vanished completely in a great gloom, black as pitch.
Not wishing that we, who know Him, should suffer further torment,
Our Lord, filled with mercy for us, ordained that the dreadful   150
Smoke should fall upon the very ones that had created it.
Then Mars bestirred himself and aroused heated battle frenzy:[37]
And then, two standard-bearers rushed out of the good city.
Each one carried a lance, and they climbed up the tower, holding
The standards, tinted golden with saffron, that frightened the Danes;[38]
A hundred of them were struck down by a hundred quick arrows—
The life of the Danes spurted away along with their blood—
Dragged off by the hair, to their ships—their last abode.
Thus was the surging of Lemnos overcome by the great might
Of Neptune—for the water soaked what the fire had ravaged.[39]   160
And there fell Rotbert, ever happy, joyful, struck down by[40]
A cruel stroke, delivered by this most pernicious people;
By God's grace, only some of our people perished with him.
Now, just as an overconfident wolf that is filled with shame,
For it seized no prey, seeks out the depths of the forest, thus did
The foe fall back and scurry away in great and furtive flight;
They mourned three hundred of their own, left lifeless for Charon.[41]
The night passed in fixing the damage done to the tower.
These two battles were fought just a few days before November
Grew frosty and ran its complete course, and just as December   170
Stood ready to wane and yield to the last days of the year.

Now as the sun began to fill the sky with reddening beams,
Over the See of the holy Dénis, up along the banks
Of the Sequanus, indeed not far from Saint-Germain-le-Rond,
The Danes assembled that they might set up their encampment,
Fashioning stakes, gathering stones and earth to pile in one heap.[42]
Then, the cruel ones, both on horseback and on foot overran
The hills, the fields, forests, open pastures and the villages.
All infants, boys and girls, youths, and even those hoary with age,
The father and the sons and even mothers—they killed them all.   180
They slaughtered the husband before the very eyes of his wife;

Coniugis ante oculos strages gustat mulierem,
Ante patrum faciem soboles necnon genitricum.
Efficitur servus liber, liber quoque servus,
Vernaque fit dominus, contra dominus quoque verna.
Vinitor agricolaeque simul cum vitibus omnes
Ac tellure ferunt crudeles mortis habenas.
Francia iam dominisque dolet famulisque relicta,
Heroe gaudebat nullo, lacrimisque rigatur.
Nulla domus stabilis vivo regitur dominante.   190
A, tellus opulenta gazis nudatur opimis,
Sanguivomis, laceris, atris, aedacibus, aequo
Vulneribus, praedis, necibus, flammis, laniatu,
Prosternunt, spoliant, perimunt, urunt, populantur,
Dira cohors, funesta falanx cetusque severus.
Posse favebat eis actutum velle quod ipsum;
Omnia se visum gestabant ante cruentum.
Valles diffugiunt humiles, tumidi prius Alpes.
Arma simul diamant lucos cum corde fugaci.
Nemo patet, fugiunt omnes, heu, nemo resistit.   200
Sic decus, a, regni pro posse tulere venusti,
Sic celebris specimen cimbis portant regionis.
Terribiles inter acies tamen adstitit acta
Parisius ridens media inperterrita tela.

Ergo bis octonis faciunt—mirabile visu—
Monstra rotis, ignara modi, conpacta triadi,
Roboris ingentis, super argete quodque cubante
Domate sublimi cooperto. Nam capiebant
Claustra sinus, archana uteri, penetralia ventris,
Sexaginta viros, ut adest rumor, galeatos.   210
Unius obtinuere modum formae satis amplae.
Completis autem geminis, ternum peragendo
Mittitur arte fala vexare falarica binos
Artifices, nervis iaculata, uno quoque plectro.
Sic nobis loetum primi meruere paratum.
Mox monade necata obiit saevissima dias.
Mille struunt etiam celsis tentoria rebus
Tergoribus collo demptis tergoque iuvencum—
Bis binos tressisve viros clipeare valebant—

Before the eyes of the husband, the wife fell prey to carnage.
The children perished right before the eyes of their parents.
The bondsman was set free, while the freeman was made a bondsman;
The slave was made the master, and the master became the slave.
Both the wine-grower and also the farmer, together with
The vineyards and the fields suffered the pitiless weight of death.
Then did the land of the Franks know grief, for masters and servants
Were gone; and gone the joy of heroes; only tears remained.
No more houses were left ruled over by a living master.   190
Alas! A rich land stripped of its treasures, left with bloody wounds,
Fully robbed, filled with grim murder—a frenzy beyond compare.
The Danes ransacked and despoiled, massacred, and burned and ravaged;
They were an evil cohort, a deadly phalanx, a grim horde.
Nor did they tarry for long to do all that they sought to do,
Being driven by some blood-filled vision that was before them.
Valleys were worn down, befouled, that were once splendid as the Alps.[43]
The men in arms, in their keenness to flee, sought out the woods.

No one stayed to be found; everyone fled. Alas! None fought back.[44]   200
Ah, the Danes took away on their ships, all that was splendid
In this good realm, all that was the pride of this famous region!
Throughout this horrible conflict, Paris stood firm, fearless;
It remained cheerful, despite all the darts that fell around it.

At this point—an astounding sight—the Danes began to construct
Sixteen monstrous wheels, as never before seen, grouped into threes;
Made of sturdy oak, each wheel had a battering ram, shielded[45]
By a roof. Now, it was within the secret hiding places,
Found all along the sides of these huge wheels, that men were concealed,
As is told, there were sixty men, girt in their helmets.   210
They had hardly finished building one of these huge siege-engines,
When, without delay, they began on the second, then the third.
Then from the tower was launched a javelin, shot with great force
And accuracy, which struck two of the Danes building these wheels.
Thus was death dealt out to those, who were preparing death for us.
The two Danes, victims of this sole attack, died not long after.[46]
Then, from the skins taken from the shoulders and necks of young bulls,
Large enough to protect three or four men, just like a big shield,
The Danes fashioned a thousand tents, held aloft by upright poles.[47]

Quae pluteos calamus vocitat cratesve latinus.   220
Nox nullam recipit requiem nullumque soporem.
Veloces acuunt, reparant, cuduntque sagittas;
Expediunt clipeos, veteresque novi efficiuntur.

Cumque senis Foebi fulgor iam scandit in almas
Quadrigas agilis noctemque repellit opacam
Atque suos oriens oculos demittit in urbem,
En proles Satanae subito castris furibundae
Erumpunt, trepidis nimium telis oneratae.
Ad turrim properant, tenues ut apes sua regna
Distentis adeunt humeris casiaque thimoque   230
Arboreisque simul vel ameni floribus agri.
Haud secus infelix populus contendit ad arcem
Pressis fornicibus humeris ferroque tremente.
Ensibus arva tegunt, Sequanam clipeis, et in urbem
Plumbea mille volant fusa densissime mala
Atque serunt pontes validis speculas catapultis.
Mars hinc inde furit surgens regnatque superbus.
Totius ecclesiae convexa boando metalla
Flebilibus vacuas supplent clamoribus auras.
Arcs nutat, cives trepidant, ingensque tubarum   240
Vox resonat, cunctosque pavor cum turribus intrat.
Hic proceres multi fortesque viri renitebant.
Antistes Gozlinus erat primas super omnes;
Huic erat Ebolusque nepos Mavortius abba.
Hic Rotbertus, Odo, Ragenarius, Utto, Erilangus,
Hi comites cuncti; sed nobilior fuit Odo,
Qui totidem Danos perimit, quot spicula mittit.
Dimicat infelix populus pugnatque benignus.
Tres armavit atrox cuneos, quibus obtulit arci
Maiorem, picto ponti geminosque parone,   250
Hanc sat opinati superare, hunc si potuissent.
Haec bellum patitur, multo maiora sed ille.
Haec depicta gemit vario sub vulnere rubra,
Ille virum luget vires obitusque fluentes.
Sanguine nulla via urbis adest intacta virorum,
Prospiciens turrisque nichil sub se nisi picta
Scuta videt; tellus ab eis obtecta latebat.

These are called *pluteos* or *crates* by one Latin writer.[48]   220
And that night imparted neither respite nor any repose,
For very hastily arrows were sharpened, repaired, forged,
And bucklers were all sorted out; even old arms were restored.

Now when Phoebus, ancient and far-shining, climbed into his prized
And swift four-horsed chariot, he drove back the darkness of night;[49]
Thereat, as he arose, his eyes fell upon the city,
Towards which surged that race of Satan from their encampment,[50]
And with frightful fury discharged murderous arrows at us.
They dashed out—headed straight for the tower, just like honeybees
Keen to return to their own land, wings filled with rosemary,   230
Thyme, and those flowers they sought out on trees and in charming fields.
Thus did these wretched people seem as they ran to the fortress,
With bows jutting from shoulders, iron-tipped arrows quivering.[51]
Their swords veiled the meadows and their bucklers hid the Seine;
Into the city they hurled a thousand pots of molten lead,
And the turrets on the bridges were knocked down by catapults.[52]
Thus did Mars stir up his furor and reign supreme over all.
Cambered church bells, that were made of bronze, stridently resounded—
Their loud peals filled the air with a dolorous clangor.
The citadel tottered, citizens grew alarmed, trumpet blasts   240
Rang—dread filled each heart—especially of those in the tower.
Then did everyone remark, both the highborn and the heroes,
That the foremost among them that day was the prelate Gozlin;
And after him, his nephew, Ebolus the abbot, favored
By Mars, and Rotbert, Odo, Ragenar, Utto, Erilang.[53]
Counts all—but the most noble among them was indeed Odo,
For it was he who shot the arrows that slew so many Danes.
The unfortunate people now fought and defended themselves.
Frenzied, the Danes formed into three corps; one charged at the tower;
The other two, boarded painted ships, and headed for the bridge;[54]   250
They thought that by winning the one they would secure the other:
The tower was struck hard; harder still the blow dealt to the bridge.
The tower groaned and was stained red with blood; often was it struck.
The bridge wept over the warriors that were swept away and died.
No path to the city was left unstained by the blood of men.
Looking down below from the tower nothing could be seen but
Painted shields; so many that the ground was completely hidden.

Inde super cernens lapides conspexit acerbos
Ac diras ut apes dense tranare cateias.
Inter sese aliud turrimque nihil metit aether.   260
Vox inmensa, metus maior, strepitusque fit altus.
Hi bellant, isti pugnant, resonantibus armis.
Praelia Normanni exacuunt crudelia sane.
Nullus habet terrae totidem qui vivere natus
Indutos gladiis pedites spectaret in unum
Et tanta miraretur testudine picta.
Hac sibi confecere polum, vitam nutrientem,
Quem nullum superare caput cupiebat eorum,
Ast infra capiunt tetre necis arma frequenter.
Mille dabant pugnam pariter stantes in agone,   270
Mille simul, turrim quoniam contingere cuncti
Haud una poterant, turmis certare studebant.
Arcs speculans, nudis quoniam chelis inimicus
Ingeminat populus certamen et ore patenti,
Erectas taxos arcus convertit in uncos.
Unius hinc iaculum transmittitur os in apertum,
Quem subito conans alius clipeare migrantem,
Nempe cibum gustat primus quem repserat ore.
Adveniens autem, numerum qui clauderet almum,
Hos nitens geminos auferre latenter, et ipse,   280
Perculsus faretra turri veniam quoque poscit.
Sub clipeis illos alii conduntque trahuntque,
Unde furore nimis pingues bellum renovarunt.
Scuta cient planctus saxis ferientibus ipsa
Sanguineasque vomunt voces galeae subeuntes
Aethera. Crudeli lorica mucrone foratur.
Respiciensque suas et quos fundaverat artus
Omnipotens fabricas modicum Danis superari,
Exhibuit nostris vires animosque valentes,
Inpertitus eis sensus equidem tremebundos.   290
Tum pereunt miseri, pluresque vehuntur ad altos
Ponentes animas torquentibus arma faselos.
Iam Titan celeres missos praemittere curat
Ocaeano, pompare thoros, otium quibus abdat.
Torvaque plebs quae iam cecini tentoria turri
Texta tulit silvis flenti caesisque iuvencis,

And up above only merciless stones were discernible,
While all about dreadful arrows flew thick as a swarm of bees.[55]
Nothing else was visible between the sky and the tower.   260
A tumult of voices arose—a ghastly noise that brought dread.
They attacked; the others fought back; the clash of arms resounded.
Hard and brutal, indeed, were the Vikings in that grim combat.
No living man, born upon this vast earth, has ever witnessed
So many foot soldiers, bearing swords, gathered in one place;
Nor has a man been more startled at their advance, behind
Painted shields held up above to form a life-preserving vault;
Not one among them dared lift his head out from under it.[56]
And yet underneath they felt constant blows that brought them black death.
A thousand gave battle, stood shoulder-to-shoulder in the fight.   270
And a thousand others, who could not overwhelm the tower,
Sought ways to batter it down by forming into smaller groups.
When the garrison of the citadel saw the hostile host
Greatly intensify the attack, all bare-armed and bare-backed,
They took up yew shafts, straight and firm, worked them into curving bows,
With which they shot arrows—and one pierced a man's open mouth.
Most hurriedly a comrade sought to protect him with his shield,
Who got to taste the same fare rammed into his friend's open mouth.
Then, a third man ran forth, making it a Trinity of sorts,[57]
Who struggled to pull the other two away, but he himself   280
Was struck down by an arrow and asked the tower for pardon.
Others dragged off the three, taking cover behind their shields.
And then the foe, filled with great rage, began the battle again.
Shields let forth their lamentations as stones struck upon them;
Helmets, trembling in the air, spewed out a blood-soaked clatter;
Cuirasses were struck and pierced by pitiless, keen-edged points.
Then did the Almighty turn His eyes upon His creation,
And upon those who were His creatures, sorely pressed by the Danes—
He revived our failing spirits; strengthened our resolve,
And over our foes He cast a presentment of great dread.   290
Then the wretched foe perished, fell beneath the hammer of arms;
Those bereft of souls were carried off to their high-prowed ships.
The Titan sun then sent its swift heralds to the ocean's edge,
Where a couch might be made ready for its hidden repose.
As I yet sang, that grim race brought tents to the woeful tower[58]
That were made of forest-wood and hides of slaughtered young oxen,

Quis noctem quidam bello quidamque sopore
Praeteriere, quibus circumtrivere meatus
Pennivolas acies vibrari felle madentes,
Militibus noctu eximiam cernentibus arcem.   300

Mane quidem flagrante novant certamina plenis
Arma trucum terris fixa testudine giro.
Certabant plures; alii fossata studere,
Quae circa resident illam, sulcosque replere;
Hinc glebas specubus frondesque dabant nemorosas,
Atque suo segetes etiam fetu viduatas,
Prata simul, virgulta quoque, et vites sine gemmis,
Hincque senes tauros pulchrasque boves vitulosque,
Postremumque necant elegos, heu, quos retinebant
Captivos, sulcisque cavis haec cuncta ferebant,   310
Idque die tota stantes agitant in agone.
Hocce pius cernens praesul clara lacrymando
Voce vocat Domini Salvatorisque parentem:
"Alma redemptoris genetrix mundique salutis,
Stella maris fulgens cunctis praeclarior astris,
Cede tuas praecibus clemens aures rogitantis.
Si tibi me libeat missas umquam celebrare,
Impius atque ferox saevus crudelis et atrox
Captivos perimens, laqueo necis inretiatur."
Arce repente volans telum deferre sategit   320
Antistes Gozlinus huic quod flendo precatur,
Qui vinctos vinctus mortis dimisit habenis,
Atque miser sociis tendit clipeumque pedemque.
Os solvit, virtute ruit sulcosque replevit
Mensurans terram, spirans animam male natam,
Captivos iuxta tritos gladio nimis eius.

Urbs in honore micat celsae sacrata Mariae,
Auxilio cuius fruimur vita modo tuti;
Hinc indicibiles illi, si forte valemus,
Reddamus grates, placidas reboemus et odas,   330
Vox excelsa tonet laudesque sonet, quia dignum:

"Pulchra parens salve Domini, regina polorum,

Which allowed some to pass the night in battle, while others slept.
Still others cut holes in the hides through which they shot swift arrows,
Finely fledged and with points steeped in bitter gall, at the warriors[59]
Who, through the night, stood as guards upon that glorious tower.   300

Now when morning began to shine, the weapons of these hard men
Again clashed; they advanced, hard-packed, underneath a *testudo*.[60]
Many of them fought; others commenced to deal with the ditches
That encircled the tower; took to filling in the trenches:
They threw in clods of earth, and leaves torn from well-wooded forests,
And stalks that they had taken and stripped utterly of all grain.
Also, they flung in hay from meadows, scrub, and vines, grapes torn off;
Then they pushed in old oxen, and even lovely cows and calves;
And lastly, alas, they slaughtered the luckless captives they held;
All this they took and piled into the trenches to fill them in.[61]   310
This is what they did the whole day through on the field of battle.
Seeing everything, the holy bishop then shed bright tears.
In a loud voice, he besought the Mother of our Lord and
Savior: "Blessed Mother of our Redeemer—sole hope
Of this world, bright Star of the Sea, brighter far than all the stars—
Bend thine ear, in mercy, to my prayers and to my pleas.
If it is thy pleasure that I again celebrate the Mass,
Grant that this foe—impious, fierce, cruel and most wicked,
That has slain the captives—be led, I pray, into death's grim noose."
Then swiftly the bishop, Gozlin, with a tearful prayer,   320
From the high tower, let loose an arrow at a Dane below,
Sending that wretch, who had dispatched others, into death's dark bonds—
The luckless man held up his shield; sought to rush to his friends;
His mouth slackened and he fell heavily; gone was all courage;
He breathed out his soul, born of evil, and stretched out on the earth,
Filling the ditch just like the very victims of his cruel sword.[62]

The city has honor through its love for Mary, most holy,
By whose grace we spend the days of our lives in harmony.
It is most fitting, while we are able, to render her thanks;
With our hymns of peace let us sing to her glory divine;   330
Let our voices ring on high; it is mete for so to do:

"O Mother most fair of our Savior. Hail, Queen of Heaven.

Nostra nites altrix, orbis constas dominatrix;
Quae saevis manibus Danum gladioque minace
Solvere Luteciae plebem dignata fuisti,
Luteciaeque satis poteras conferre salutem,
Quae lubrico Salvatorem cosmo genuisti.
Caelicoli caetus, virtutes ac dominatus,
Primatusque potestatesque thronique polorum,
O genetrix sobolis summi regis celebranda,   340
Te gaudent, recolunt, laudant, venerantur, adorant.
O felix, uteri thalamo quae claudere mater,
Quem coeli nequeunt, tellus, vastum mare, quisti,
Atque tuum delecta patrem nobis peperisti.
Luna micans solem multo plus te renitentem
Fudisti terries, et eas quo plena manebas
Inradiando, genus nostri lapsum reparasti.
Ergo cui, regina poli, conponere quibo?
Sanctior es cunctis, sexu felicior omni.
Cultorum miserere tui, iam nata potentis.   350
Gloria, laus et honor radiansque decus tibi semper
Sit, benedicta Dei mater, sceptris in Iesu."

Foebus abit, noctisque redit caligo serenae,
Excubiisque nequam turris saepitur opimis.
Aurora girante polos girantur et arces,
Mortiferis siquidem telis quatientibus illas.
Arrietes conflant, unumque locant ab eoo
In turrim, contemplatur septentrio celsa
In portas alium; tenuit contra latus eius
Oc que cidens ternum. Magno cum pondere nostri   360
Tigna parant, quorum calibis dens summa peragrat,
Machina quo citius Danum quisset terebrari.
Conficiunt longis aeque lignis geminatis
Mangana quae proprio vulgi libitu vocitantur;
Saxa quibus iaciunt ingentia, sed iaculando
Allidunt humiles scaenas gentis truculentae.
Sepe quidem cerebrum cervice trahunt elegorum,
Vah, multosque terunt Danos, plures quoque peltas.
Immunis clipeus fractu nullus fuit, ictus

Thou shinest as our Sustainer; art Ruler of this world.
From the hateful hand and most cruel sword of the Danes thou hast,
In thy mercy, delivered us, the people of Lutetia.
Without effort hast thou brought deliverance to Lutetia,
Just as thou didst bring forth a Savior for this fallen world.
Thus hosts of high heaven, the Virtues, and the Dominions,
The Principalities, the Powers, and the Thrones found above—[63]
O Mother of the King of Glory and most worthy of praise—   340
All these delight in thee, they revere, laud, adore, praise thee.
O blessed Mother, that which came to be contained in thy womb,
That which neither heaven, nor earth, nor yet the vast sea could hold,
Was thine own Maker; thou wert chosen to give Him birth for us.
O Bright Moon, thou hast brought forth a Sun far brighter than thyself
For this our earth—that bright Sun which filled thee to completion.
Thou didst bring salvation to our kind, who had sore fallen.
Now, with whom shall I compare Thee, O Queen of lofty Heaven?
Holier than the saints art thou; more blessed than all women.
On thy devotees have mercy, Daughter of the Almighty.   350
May all glory, all laud and honor shine around thee always.
Blessed be the Mother of God in the Kingdom of Jesus."[64]

In the year 886.
Phoebus departed; night returned with its darkness and silence,
Throngs of the grim enemy crowded round about the tower:
When Aurora circled the sky, the foe circled the tower.
Death-dealing arrows struck the Danes grimly; all but destroyed them.
Still they pushed forward the battering rams—one at the East side,
Hard against the tower; another North by the seven hills,[65]
Up against the gates; and a third stationed at the Western part.
All the while, our men made ready hefty shafts of hard wood,   360
Each one pierced at the far end with a keen tooth of iron,
With which to strike rapidly at the siege engines of the Danes.
With thick planks, doubled and of equal length, our men swiftly
Constructed *mangonels*, as they are known in the common tongue,[66]
From which they shot forth great, massive stones that landed cruelly,
Smashing utterly the humble shelters of the vile Danes;
The brains of those wretches were battered out of their skulls.
Yes, many were the Danes that were crushed, and many the shields smashed;
For no shield pummeled and battered so very hard can survive,

Quem talis tetigit, non ullus morte misellus. 370
Ast infelices foveas supplere falanges
Nequiquam tendunt, potuere replere nec ullam.
Nitebantur enim arietibus pessumdare turrim.
Quos quoniam nequeunt aequis deducere campis,
Corripiunt ternas rabidi kimbas satis altas,
Frondivagis equidem silvis gravidare flagrantes;
Postremum Vulcanus eis inponitur ardens.
Flammivomas oriens dimittit eas pedetemptim.
Anquinisque trahebantur ripas secus ipsae
Ad pontem seu conspicuam conburere turrim. 380
Silva vomit flammas, arent latices pelagique,
Terra gemit, virides herbae moriuntur ab igni.
Lemnius atque potens Neptuno stat pede trito,
Regna poli furvus penetrat nubesque peragrat.
Hinc tellus et ager, limfae caelique cremantur.
Urbs luget speculaeque timent et menia deflent.
Heu, quam magna oculis manant lacrimosa beatis
Flumina. Dant pulchri iuvenes, sed et alba senectus,
Merentes gemitus; matresque iubas laniando
Terga dabant siccae, crinesque per arva revolvunt. 390
Hae colafis nudata suis iam pectora tundunt;
At secuere genas aliae lacrimis madefactas.
Tum trepidant cives, cunctique vocant celebrandum
Germanum: "Miserere tuis, Germane, misellis."
Parisius praesul fuerat sanctissimus olim,
Inlustrabat eam cuius venerabile corpus.
Menia Germani nomen recinunt, et in omni
Exclamat miles specula primique virorum:
"O famulis, Germane, tuis succurrere disce."
Littora seu liquidi laticis pelagus ciet altum, 400
Sidereosque thronos, quibus emicat ut iubar almus,
Verberat innumerus, echo comitante, boatus;
Germanum respondet et urbs vocitantibus ipsum.
Concurrunt matres pariter iuvenesque puellae
Ad sancti tumulum, suffragia poscere grata.
Infelix et ob hoc populus subiit nimis alta
Gaudia, subsannans cives Dominique catervam.
Scuta dabant alapis reprobo risu saturatis,

Nor can a vile wretch ever hope to escape crushing death.   370
In vain their hapless phalanxes rushed to fill the ditches;
However, not even one could they succeed in filling up.
They sought to destroy the tower with blows from battering rams;
They could not easily drag these over the level terrain.
In a furious rage, they got hold of three rowing vessels,
Which they loaded full with forests of branches and mounds of leaves,
And then on these they brought on board Vulcan, fiercely burning.
Spewing flames, these ships slowly began to drift from East to West;
They were guided and pulled by taut ropes along the river bank:
The enemy hoped either to burn the bridge or the tower.   380
The blazing wood belched flames; the river's current and waves dried up;
The earth groaned, as the wild conflagration charred the green grasses.
The mighty god of Lemnos trampled frail Neptune underfoot—
His dark pall was flung wide, and covered the sky, and hid the clouds.
The land, the meadows, the water, the sky were all set ablaze;
The city lamented, the guards on the towers mourned; walls wept.[67]
Alas, great was the outburst of tears from many blessed
Eyes. Handsome youths along with grizzled old men groaned and let loose
Great lamentations, while mothers, though dry-eyed, yet tore and snatched
At their hair—pulled out locks stirred in the dust of the fields.   390
Some women bared their breasts; struck at them with beating fists,
While others scratched their cheeks, already bedewed with tears.
Fearful, the men of the city cried out to the famed Saint
Germain: "Have mercy, O Germain, on us your luckless children."[68]
He had been the bishop of Paris once—was deemed the holiest;
His revered body is a bright shining light for the city.
The ramparts resounded with the name of Germain, and on each
Tower the warriors, and the highborn who led them, shouted:
"O Germain, hear our cry; help us, your steadfast servants."
The many-throated cry swept down the banks and stirred the river's   400
Deep-flowing depth, and ceaseless echoes arose to the starry
Thrones, where the Saint resides lustrous like the bright Morning Star;
The city swelled these echoes with more cries to their Germain.
Mothers and young maids ran together, in a great multitude,
To the Saint's holy tomb, there to plead for his kind succor.
Now, the faithless foes looked upon all this with growing pleasure,
And they ridiculed the inhabitants and the Lord's army;
With mocking laughter they banged their shields loud with open hands;

Argutoque tument horum distenta boatu
Guttura, et urbanis plangentibus aera magno   410
Implentur sonitu, clamore minus nihil amplo;
Vox auditur in excelsis et luctus in aethris.
At Deus omnipotens omnis fabricae raeparator
Orbis, adest precibus sancti rogitatus, et ipse,
O Germane, venis humili succurrere plebi
Auxilio, lapidumque salire struem super altam
Flammivomas puppes, pontem ne lederet ulla,
Ipse coegisti; pontem sustentat is agger.
Continuo Domini populus descendit ad ignes,
Quos mergens in aquas, naves cepit sibi victor;   420
Hincque Dei sumpsit felix gaudere caterva,
Unde prius duxit gemitus magnosque dolores
Sic nostris geritur, bellumque diesque recedit,
Noxque falam gurdis mandat custodibus ipsam.
Sole suas nondum claras subeunte quadrigas,
Sub lucem reveunt crates sua ad oppida furtim,
Arrietes carcamusas vulgo resonatos
Dimisere duos, pallos vetuit removere,
Quos nostri capiunt gaudenter depeculantes.
Rexque Danos retulit Sigenfredus super omnes,   430
Quem turris metuit proprios sibi vellere ocellos.
Sicque iuvante Deo dirus Mavors requievit.
Ianuarii suprema dies statuit triduana;
Haec finire sequens studuit certamina mensis.
Tercia lux huius fuerat belli recolendae
Sancta genetricis tunc purificatio Christi,
Quae nostrae tribuit plebi gaudere triumpho.

Praeterea conscendit equos avibus otiores
Infortuna cohors, repetens partes orientis,
Francia quas nondum populatas tristis alebat.   440
Cuncta prius dimissa necans magalia poscit
Quae Rotberto aderant Faretrato agnomine claro,
Cuius erat miles tantum obsequio modo solus.
Una domus retinebat eos. Miles seniori:
"Normannos contemplor," ait, "cursim venientes."
Rotbertusque suum cupiens admittere scutum

Their throats swelled and strained as they shouted out odious cries.
And the people of the city let forth great moans; with loud cries   410
The air was rent, not less strident than the din of the foe.
Their shouts were heard on high; our grief rose up to heaven.
Then, God the Omnipotent, the Savior of all the world
Lent His ear to the prayers and pleadings of His saint. And
You, O Germain, came to the succor of your humble people
That were laid low. You drove the fire-spewing vessels to crash
Against a high heap of stones, so that no harm came to the bridge;
This pile of stones was built up to give more support to the bridge.
Then hastily ran the people of God down to the fires
And doused them with river-water—they kept the ships as plunder.   420
Thus did the jubilant host of the Lord snatch up great gladness
From these fire-ships that earlier brought them sorrow and grief.
And our men fought on; and the battle ended with the day.
At night, the foe placed a few reckless men around the tower.
The sun had yet to mount its far-shining four-horsed chariot
When, near dawn, they slyly brought carts and cats to the city;[69]
Two battering-rams, or *carcamusa* in the vulgar tongue,[70]
They left unguarded and were too afraid to return for them—
So our men got hold of these two rams and made off with them.
Then, King Siegfried ordered the Danes to retreat. Above all men,   430
He was most prone to gouge out the tower's eyes—that is, its gates.[71]
Thus, by the grace of God, savage Mars allowed us some respite.
This strife had lasted through the last three days of January,
And the month that followed sought to bring an end to the conflict.
Now the third day of battle had also fallen on the Feast
Of the Purification of the Blessed Mother of Christ—
And so she allowed our people to rejoice in triumph.[72]

Now, the cohorts of the faithless fiends mounted their horses that
Were swifter than birds, and headed out for the Eastern regions,[73]
The only portions of poor France that had not been ravaged.   440
They killed those that were left behind, and then they sought the dwellings
Belonging to the famed Rotbert the Quiver, as he was called.[74]
With him stood but one trustworthy and devoted warrior.
They were both inside a house. Then the warrior said to him:
"I can make out the Norsemen," he stated, "they come at a charge."
And then, Rotbert went looking for his shield, but he found it not;

Nil vidit, populus quoniam suus abstulit illud,
Quem Danicos iussit cuneos idem speculari.
Ense forum nudo petiit tamen obvius illis,
E quibus occidit geminos, et tertius ipse   450
Incubuit morti, nullo sibi subveniente.
Unde nepos eius nimium tristans Adalaelmus
Consulis intererat populo, cui talia dixit:
"Eia, viri fortes, clipeos sumatis et arma,
Ulciscique meum raptim properemus avunculum."
Haec inquit, villam petiit, congressus acerbis
Ilicet hos vicitque trucidavitque nefandos.
Normanno villam victor moriente replevit.
Nil reliqui, prohibente fuga retulere paroni.
Haec eadem Rotbertus erat nitens operari.   460

Post aequor residens almi niveam secus aulam
Scandere Germani temptant crebrius vocitati,
Eius qua speciem constat lucere sepulchri.
Hic iacuit suimet iugiter venerabile corpus,
Nobiliusque monasterium cunctis fuit illud,
Nustria quae refovere sinu discebat in amplo.
Hinc propriis fuerit famulis gestatus in urbem.
Ipse Danos, quicumque dabant vestigia prato,
Militibus speculam cernentibus urbis in eius
Rure sitam fugiente mora tradit capiendos.   470
Ecclesiam cuius penetrans lacerare fenestras
Ictibus arboreis unus vitreas lanionum,
Continuo amenti rabie confunditur atrox,
Curribus Eumenidum piceis artatus ab almo,
Morsque sequens miserum perdit, pietate remota,
Hisque fatigatus causis inferna petivit.
Mi Germane sacer, cura ne spiritus olim
Illa meus subeat, cuius miracula canto.
Haec et quo supplere queam, faveas precor, alme;
Summa patris summi natique, rogato, columba   480
Ore meo sedeat, mentem repleat, pie domne,
Actibus atque sacris virtutum floribus ornet,
Expulsis sestrice sacra vitiis procul atris.

Now, one of his own men had taken it away when he gave
The command to go and keep watch on the movements of the Danes.
With only his bare sword in hand, he went out to face them:
Two he slew at once, but the third one to fall was he himself.　　450
Thus was he carried off by death, for no one came to his aid.
This was a cause for great sorrow for his nephew Adalhelm,[75]
Who went and stood among Rotbert's men; spoke to them in this way:
"Come, stout-hearted warriors, let us take our shields and arms,
And let us hasten to seek revenge for my noble uncle."
Thus he spoke. Then he made for those dwellings to meet the grim foe.
Forthwith, he slaughtered them, vanquished them, routed those evil fiends.
Triumphant, he piled that place high with the dead of the Norsemen.
The rest carried nothing to their ships, for flight busied them.
And such were the deeds that Rotbert himself would have accomplished.　　460

Then, the Danes sought to overrun the meadow that stretches out
In front of the radiant church of Germain, mentioned before,
Wherein his bright, resplendent sepulcher has always stood.[76]
Through the many years, his holy body has lain there.
And noble is his monastery, far more than all others
That are to be found being nourished at vast Neustria's breast;
There the faithful placed him when they brought his body to Paris.
He drove away any Dane that might set foot on his meadow—
Out towards his tower, on which stood good warriors as guards,
Who then fell upon a Dane and took him captive most quickly.　　470
One Dane broke into the Saint's church; dared to shatter the glass
Placed in all the windows, with a cudgel made from a tree-branch.
When he came out to the meadow, a seething madness gripped him,
And the Saint hitched him to the grim cart of the Eumenides;[77]
Then, death soon came upon him, without mercy, and laid him low;
Drained off all his strength and dragged the sorry wretch down into Hell.
O blessed Germain, let not my spirit, one day, fall into
That horrid abyss, for I ever sing of your miracles.
And may these miracles grant me strength to sing with purity.
Pray for me, Master, that the Father, Son, and Holy Spirit　　480
May aid my tongue and my lips, and may fill my mind completely,
That holy deeds, flowers of virtue, may be its adornment,
And the loathsome darkness of sin may be driven far away.

Torriculi scandens alius sublime cacumen,
Mutat iter per quod subiit, gressus quoque volvit
Ardua praecelsi nimium per culmina templi;
Ossa cui fregere sacri fastigia tecti,
Germani meritis urgentibus. Hoc super urbis
Pergama stans venturus Odo rex prodidit omni
Stipanti semet plebi, digito manifestans.   490
Ipse Danum semet retulit vidisse cadentem.
Tercius adveniens oculos direxit in amplum
Mausoleum sancti, nolens quos liquit ibidem.
Quod subiens quartus superis est demptus ab auris
Obticuitque sub occidua mox sorte sopitus.
Fortunate, tui quintus, Germane, parentis
Accelerat reserare thorum; primo sed adempto
Percutit hinc saxo proprium pectus, patientem
A cathedra cogens animam decedere pestis,
Quae nolens baratri tetigit caenacula tetri.   500
Inlustrem sobolis sanctae servat genitorem
Dextera, leva sacram prolis retinet genetricem.
Est Eleutherius pater, est Eusebia mater.

Pro dolor. En medius cecidit pons nocte silenti
Obsitus alluviis tumida bachantibus ira.
Nam sparsim Sequana circumfudit sua regna
Exuviisque suis obtexerat aequora campum.
Australis gestabat eum vertex, sed et arcem
Quae tellure manet sancti fundata boati.
Urbis inherebant dextris, alter sed et altri.   510
Mane quidem surgente Dani surgunt simul acres
Atque rates subeunt, armis onerant clipeisque,
Transque natant Sequanam, turrim cinguntque misellam.
Multa dabant illi densis certamina telis.
Urbs tremuit lituique boant lacrimisque rigantur
Moenia, rusque gemit totum pelagusque remugit.
Aera circumeunt lapides et spicula mixtim.
Exclamant nostri clamantque Dani; simul omnis
Terra tremit; nostri lugent, laetantur et illi.
Dumque volunt, cives nequeunt succurrere turri   520
Atque viris bello deferre iuvamen anhelis,

Now, a Dane clambered right up the soaring spire of the church;[78]
Misjudging his way, he placed his foot on the sharp abutment,
And down he tumbled; rolled off the steep-pitched summit of the church;
The holy roof of the church utterly shattered all his bones—
This was none but Germain's doing. On the city walls Odo,
The future king, brought attention to what had just come to pass,
Pointed it out with his finger, to those gathered around him. 490
He told them that with his own eyes he saw the Dane tumble down.
Then, a third Dane rushed forward; he had his eyes set on the vast
Sepulcher of the Saint—truly, this was his very last sight.
Next, a fourth Dane came up, but the wind knocked him down from on high,
And soon enough he was swept into the silent sleep of death.
Then, a fifth Dane, O blessed Germain, hurried to pry open
The tomb of your father—but the very first stone he loosened
Hit him hard, right on the chest. This deadly blow impelled his soul
To forsake its despicable abode and make its ways down,
Reluctantly, to nibble the dismal feast served up in Hell. 500
To the right lies the illustrious father of this blessed son,
And to the left lies the pious, holy mother of this son;
Eleutherius was his father; Eusebia his mother.[79]

Alas, at the still of night the mid-section of the bridge broke;
It was pulled apart by the raging frenzy of the current—[80]
For the Seine had broken its banks and broadened wide its domain,
And swathed the plain with water and debris—spoils of its triumph.
The bridge was supported by the hillock to the South, just like
The tower, and both stood in the domain of the blessed Saint—
Found to the right of the city, the one shored up the other.[81] 510
When the morning arose, the Danes hastily arose with it,
And taking their ships, they loaded them with weapons and shields,
And crossed the Seine, and then surrounded the pitiful tower.[82]
Many times the Danes struck, and thick flew the arrows and spears.
The city shuddered, horns resounded, flowing tears made wet
The ramparts. All the land groaned and the waters gave forth bellows.[83]
Stones and javelins, intermingled, flew thick through the air.
Our men shouted; the Danes cried and shrieked, while at the same time
The earth trembled. Our men mourned, while the Danes shouted with joy.
The inhabitants, though they wished to, could not help the tower, 520
Nor could they bring aid to the warriors panting in battle.

Quos valide numero bellantes sub duodeno
Rumfea vel formido Danum non terruit umquam.
Difficile est dictu bellum, sed nomina subsunt:
Ermenfredus,[2] Eriveus, Erilandus, Odaucer,
Ervic, Arnoldus, Solius, Gozbertus, Vuido,
Ardradus, pariterque Eimardus Gozsuinusque.
Seque neci plures sociarunt ex inimicis.
Hi quoniam nequeunt animis curvarier atris,
Aestibus accingunt carpentum arentibus arcis   530
Ante fores gurdi miserandae gramine plenum.
Fulmineisque velut Foebo sub rura procellis
Nox vacua celi specie confunditur alta,
Fas nulli arridente suum contemnere doma;
Haud secus occuluit fumus speculam catapultis
Inmersis aliquantisper fervore tonante.
Quisque rogi proprios flatus ne clade perirent
Accipitres loris permisit abire solutis;
Quem dum iam cupiunt omnes extinguere, desunt
Vasa, quibus possent latices haurire fluentes.   540
Namque Danum formidabant ausum fore nullum
Aequora iam confessoris contingere gressu
Pansa prius propter meritis miracula sancti.
Haud modicam retinent solum nisi quippe lagenam,
Quae, claram iaciendo focos Sequanam super altos,
Servantum fugit digitis dilapsa sub illos;
Vulcano periit claudo Neptunus inermis.
Larque super turrim saliit, contrivit et omnem.
Robora congeminant gemitus oppressa sub igni,
Plus bello dominante rogo. Dimittitur illa   550
Militibus, pontis subeunt extrema relicta.
Praelia constituunt illic nova saevaque saevis,
Donec ad alta caput flexit Foebus vada ponti.
Pila dabat rupesque simul celeresque cateias
Plebs inimica Deo, pransura Plutonis in urna;
Sed quia conflictus talis superare nequibat,
Militibus clamare: "Fidem," cepit, sed inanem,

---

[2] A reads *Ermemfredus*, which GP, PW, and HW retain. It is the Frankish name *Hermanfried*.

These warriors that fought with such valor were twelve in number,
They feared not the cruel and merciless swords of the Danes.
How they fought, it is difficult to tell, but their names are:
Hermanfried and Eriveus, Herland and Odoacer,
Herric and Arnold and Soli and Gosbert and Uvido,
As well, they had with them Hardrad and Einhard and Gozwin, too.[84]
They forced many of the enemy to walk the path of death.
The courage of these men could not be crushed by the cruel foe.
And then the Danes brought forward a wagon, piled high with dried hay;   530
They set it alight, and pushed it against the wretched tower.
Just as in the countryside, Phoebus sends down a savage storm,
And darkness fights fiercely with the light in the sky's great orb—
And no man holds back a smile of joy when he sees his own home—
A similar storm engulfed the tower, obscured it with smoke,
And for some time, the catapults were hidden by the high flames.[85]
Then did each of the twelve men loosen the jesses of his hawk
And let it soar away that it might not perish in the blaze.[86]
And then they set about to extinguish the conflagration,
But they had no buckets with which to draw water from the flow.   540
No fear had they, for they knew no Dane would dare set foot
Upon fields that belonged to the great and forceful Confessor,[87]
For already they had witnessed miracles wrought by the Saint.
Soon they got hold of a small firkin with which they could haul up
The clear water of the Seine to throw on the leaping blaze.
But this firkin slipped from their fingers; landed in the flames:
And thus defenseless Neptune surrendered to limping Vulcan.[88]
The fire leaped onto the tower; engulfed it completely.
Oppressed by the flames, the stout oaken planks further groaned greatly.
Troubled more by the blaze than by the grim fray, our twelve men   550
Forsook the tower and fell back to the far end of the bridge.
There they keenly renewed the fight against the cruel foe,
Until Phoebus turned his head towards the great depths of the sea.
These Danes, enemies of God, hurled spears, rocks, and swift arrows,
And still they all went down to eat from Pluto's bitter cauldron.[89]
But unable to be triumphant in the fight, they called out
To the twelve warriors: "We give you our oath"—falsely sworn—

"Ad nostram properare, viri, nolite timere."
Pro dolor. Alloquiis sese credunt male finctis,
Sperantes precio redimi potuisse sub amplo;　　　　　　　560
Non alias vere caperentur luce sub illa.
Heu, nudi gladium subeunt gentis truculentae,
Et caelo mittunt animas livore fluente;
Martirii palmam sumunt caramque coronam.

Mox reliquis ut visus adest gentilibus Eriveus,[3]
Rex, quoniam facie splendens formaque venustus,
Creditur atque sui donis grassante tuetur.
Protenus intuitu fuso cernendo sodales
Dilectos plecti, tamquam leo sanguine viso
Ipse furit, conansque manus vitare tenentum　　　　　　　570
Undique vi volvit semet ceu nexus, ut arma
Sumeret ulcisci proprios socialeque vulnus;
Obtentuque carens ipso sic insuperata
Limphantes potuit qua voce tonavit in aures:
"Cedite me tensa cervice; pecunia prorsus
Nulla meam tractet vitam morientibus istis.
Vivere quid sinitis? Frustratur vestra cupido."
Quae lux haud eius, micuit sed crastina flatu.
Quae voces, quae lingua, quod os edicere possunt
Bella tot his prato egregii commissa relati?　　　　　　　580
Quotque necaverunt Normannos hic? Quot et urbi
Duxerunt secum vivos? Iam nullus eorum
Tunc audebat agrum sancti conscendere latum.
Quorum, prae terrore, virum certamina promo,
Corpora crudeles Sequanae tradunt sine vita,
Laus corum iugiter nomenque per ora virorum
Insignesque simul mortes et bella volabunt,
Sol radiis donec noctis pompare tenebras,
Luna diem, stellae pariter conponere discant.
Prosternuntque dehinc speculam de morte dolentem　　　　590
Custodum. Cecidit telo quatiente Danorum
Signifer; hic artus misit flatumque Charoni.

---

[3] A reads *Erveus*, which GP, PW, and HW retain. This emendation clearly establishes this warrior to be the same one mentioned earlier in line 525.

"Come out to us, O worthy men. You have nothing to fear."
Alas, the twelve put their trust in this oath, falsely given.
Now, it was their hope to be held for a goodly ransom—   560
For on that day they would have been captured by no other means.
Ah, they fell under the naked swords of those brutal people,
And their souls rose up to heaven, as their blood flowed out.
Thus did these twelve men win the palm and the crown of martyrdom.

But one among them, Eriveus, was thought to be a king,[90]
By the Danes, for fair was his demeanor, and most noble;
They hoped he would bring a good ransom, and so treated him well.
But when he saw how his dear companions were harshly
Slaughtered, then like a lion that smells blood, did he fiercely
Rage and struggle to get loose and escape the hands that held him,   570
Like a man held in bonds, he strongly writhed and twisted about,
Seeking a weapon with which to avenge the grief of his friends.
But try as he might, he could not bring about what he wanted;
In a roaring voice, he screamed into the ears of his foes:
"Here is my neck, stretched out! Now, strike off my head! For no amount
Of money shall I ransom my life—not when they have perished!
Why do you let me live? You shall get nothing for all your greed!"
He did not die that day, but met his doom the very next day.
What words, what tongues, what mouths can tell all the deeds done in battle,
By the many doughty warriors, upon those blessed fields?   580
How many Norsemen did they slay, and how many did they take
Into the city as hostages? No Dane will now dare
To come ashore and place his foot on the wide fields of the Saint—
Such was the dread spread by the deeds of men of whom I have sung.
But their lifeless bodies the grim foes flung into the Seine—
Their fame, their names shall never cease to be on men's lips;
Their high deeds and their gallant deaths shall be remembered
Until the sun learns to gild the darkness of night with its rays,
And the moon and the stars together come to brighten the day.[91]
Then, the Danes tore down the tower that yet sorrowed at the deaths   590
Of its custodians. But an arrow struck down a Danish[92]
Standard-bearer—sending down to Charon his strength, his soul.

Nemo meis super hoc dictis insurgere bello
Decertet; siquidem nemo nil verius ullus
Expediet, quoniam propriis obtutibus hausi;
Sic etiam nobis retulit, qui interfuit ipse
Atque natando truces gladios evadere quivit.

Tum Sequanam saliunt Ligerumque petunt, patriamque
Has inter geminas peragrant praedam capientes,
Quam regio ipsa meo pandet iussu dominante.   600
Interea sperans Ebolus fortissimus abba,
Gentiles quod in hanc issent cuncti, prope solus
Arce ruit, dardumque ferens castella petivit
Illorum hastamque vibrans proiecit in ipsa;
Non sonipes retulit nobis hunc, nec tulit illuc.
Confestim socium nixus munimine saeva
Castra petit, murosque ferit; quo Lemnius adsit
Ipse iubet; pugnant nostri, constantius illi;
Argutus nimium fremitus iam fumat ab illis,
Exiliuntque foras, vulgusque fugant sine tactu,   610
Extiterant plures quoniam nobis. Tamen illis
Obvius hic Ebolus, sociique simul, stetit heros.
Haud illum fuerant audentes tangere ferro;
Quingentis etiamsi tunc subnixus adesset
Qualis et ipse fuit, castris sese daret ultro,
Ast animas propria de sede repelleret omnes.
At quia militibus caruit, sic ludere cessat.
Nustria nobilior cunctis regionibus orbis,
Quae vaste fueras procerum genetrix dominan tum,
Ne pigeat capta turri producere, quaeso,   620
Quot vel quas hausere Dani palmas tibi, necnon
Ubera quot pecorum mulsere, tuum peragrando
Distentum variis tractum gazis tamen olim.

"Mi soboles, aliquis censere potest? Etiamsi
Affuerint cunctae volucres, erumpere voces
Tot nequeunt hominum quot equum pecudumque boumque
Sublegere mihi natos natasque suumque;

Therefore, let no man speak of this fight, as if he knew more.
Indeed, no man may speak of these events more truly than I,
For I saw everything that happened with my very own eyes;
And my account agrees with the one related by a man
Who was there, and who dodged Danish swords by swimming across.[93]

Then the Danes crossed over the Seine and headed out for the Loire;[94]
They scoured the land between the two rivers for great booty.
This region will speak soon enough, at my wish, and tell its tale.   600
Now, Ebolus, that most valiant abbot, thinking that all
The heathens had departed, rushed out, alone, from the ramparts.
With spear in hand, he ran to where the Danes had been camped,
And there he brandished and flung his spear into that camp—
No courser bore him thither; neither did one carry him back.[95]
Quickly, and now with some companions by his side, he sought
The dwellings of the grim Danes. He struck the walls; bade Vulcan be
Used. Then, hard fought our men. But harder still fought back the Danes.[96]
A great roar rose from their ranks, along with smoke from the camp.
And then, more Danes appeared and swiftly put the throng to flight—   610
But they killed not one, though they were more in number. Neither could
They harm Ebolus, nor those with him—heroes against the foe.
The Danes had not the valor to touch him with their iron.
Had he but five hundred men with him, who were as brave as he,
Then, easily could he have overrun their encampment,
And parted the soul from the body of those he came across.
But he did not have such men and could not fight on for too long.
Neustria, noblest by far of all the regions of the earth,
Many worthy men have you borne that have won realms and high fame.
Do not hold back to tell, I pray you, when the tower fell, how   620
Great were the treasures the Danes got—spoils of their triumph.
How many teats of bountiful cows did they squeeze as they roved
And ranged across your broad lands that were once gorged with immense wealth.

THE VOICE OF NEUSTRIA:[97]
"My son, is it possible to relate this tale? Were all
The winged birds gathered round, their many voices would not
Be enough to speak of the men and horses, swine and oxen—
My numerous sons and daughters—that have been taken from me.
My rivers and my fields, abundant in pasture, once echoed

Flumina balatu agnorum, mea gramine laeta
Prata sonant denso mugitu tempe iuvencum,
Cervorumque nemus rauco clamore remugit,   630
Grunnitusque mei silvas scindebat aprorum.

Haec mihi subduxere truces, si noscis et audis."
Haec oculis equidem petii sistens super urbis
Moenia, nec visu claudebantur neque ritmo;
At quoniam cingi nequeunt pratis nec ab agris,
Efficitur bostar Germani antistitis aula,
Completur tauris, suculis simisque capellis.
Longa trahunt illic suspiria tumque dehiscunt,
Corpora flant dulces ventos cruciante dolore.
Adveniunt stabulatores ea ferre quoquinae   640
Nitentes, cum iam maneant epulae innumeratis
Vermibus, ecclesia quorum fetore repleta.
Exportant, Sequanae referunt, non nempe quoquinae,
Ecclesiamque piant bovibus, nec caeditur ultra.

"Legisti praedas, etiam cognosce trophea.
Restitit oppida quaeque capi suprema voluntas;
Obfuit at, Domino tribuente infirma potestas.
Carnoteno innumeros conflictus applicuerunt
Allofili, verum liquere cadavera mille
Hic, quingenta simul, rubeo populante duello.   650
Una dies istum voluit sic ludere ludum,
His ducibus, Godefredo necnon et Odone;
Belligeri fuerant Uddonis consulis ambo.
Idem Odo praeterea opposuit ne saepius illis,
Et vicit iugiter victor. Heu, liquerat illum
Dextra manus bello quondam, cuius loca cinxit
Ferrea, pene vigore nichil infirmior ipsa.
Nec satius quicquam sortiti apud hi Cinomannos;
Haud equidem reliquae cesserunt suavius urbes."
Iam, quia Apollo rogat, calamus requiem mereatur.   660

TERMINATUR PRIMUS.

With the bleating of driven sheep; my vales rang with the groans of
Young bulls; my deep groves responded with the hoarse bark of deer; 630
My many forests were filled with the hard grunts of boars. But those
Grim Danes robbed me of all these, if you will but listen and learn."

From the city walls, I saw with my eyes—and how true it was—
How much was lost could not be reckoned by sight or by number.
Since the Danes could not pen all the beasts in the fields and meadows,
They turned the sacred hall of Saint Germain into a stable,[98]
And filled it full of countless bulls, young sows, and short-headed sheep.
Long were the sighs these sad animals drew, with mouths gaping wide;
Their bodies wracked with pain when they let out their last breaths.
And when their herdsmen arrived to take them for the cookhouse, 640
They found them dead, and their bodies were infested with so
Many worms—and the church was wholly filled with their fetid stench.
They took the bodies not to the cookhouse, but down to the Seine;
To the church belonged the cows, and none could be slaughtered for food.[99]

THE VOICE OF NEUSTRIA:
"You have read how I was plundered—learn now of my great triumphs.
The chief desire of the Danes was the capture of my towns,
Yet, by the Lord's grace, our weakness became their hindrance.
These merciless strangers brought ceaseless strife to Chartres. But they
Had to leave behind a thousand corpses of their own men,
As well as five hundred more, after a battle most bloody. 650
And all this after just one day and after just one skirmish
With the battle lords Godfried and Oddo, the most valiant;
Both these warriors attended and served the high Lord Uddo.[100]
He was that Oddo who always stood firm against each assault,
And ever was the victor in each fray. Alas, already
He had lost his right hand in war, and in its place he had fixed
A hand of iron, and which was in no way any weaker.
Neither did these strangers fare any better in Le Mans,
For not one city yielded to them without difficulty.[101]
But now, Apollo beckons. Let the pen take its hard-earned rest. 660

HERE ENDS THE FIRST BOOK.

ORDITUR SECUNDUS BELLORUM PARISIACAE POLIS CODICELLUS.

Surgito Musa celer, lampas accendit eoa
Climata; luciferam propera praevertere plantam.

Saxonia vir Ainricus fortisque potensque
Venit in auxilium Gozlini, praesulis urbis,
Attribuit victus illi loetumque cruentis,
Heu paucis, auxit vitam nostris, tulit amplam
His praedam. Sub nocte igitur quadam penetravit
Castra Danum, multos et equos illic sibi cepit.
Agmen Ainrico cedente nimis lanionum,
Efficitur celsus nimium clamor fremitusque;   10
Deserit unde quies nostros, et menia vallant.
Inmodicas voces flavere Dani morientes.
Inmenso resonant cives clangore paventes
Ut solitum paterentur ab his ex more laborem.
Sic et Ainricus postremum castra reliquit,
Culpa tamen, fugiente mora, defertur ad arcem
Pila ministrabant acidas referendo salutes.
Ianua militibus reseratur, comminus acre
Urgetur bellum, clipei labuntur et enses.
Vita meos adamat dextros oditque sinistros,   20
Infestos adamat mors, vita gubernat amicos.
Inde sopor repetit cives, miserosque fugella.

Rege Sigemfredo simul ast Odone loquente,
Protenus a specula currentes agmine multo,
Ducere forte truces secum conantur Odonem;
Qui primum feriendo falae fossata volatu
Transsiliit propero clipeum gestansque cateiam.
More suo functus bello versus stetit heros;
Exiliere viri domino suffragia dantes,
Nobilibusque stupent eius super actibus omnes.   30

Conspiciens Sigemfredus nostros in agone
Esse feros, inquit sociis: "Hanc linquite sedem;
Hic non stare diu nostrum manet, hinc sed abire."

HERE BEGINS THE SECOND SMALL BOOK
OF THE BATTLES OF THE CITY OF PARIS.

Swiftly arise, O Muse, for the lamp of heaven illumines
The Eastern sky. Be quick; keep pace with that progression of light.

Heinrich, that man from Saxony, fearless and valiant,
Came to lend support to Gozlin, the bishop of the city,[102]
Bringing life to the one, and to the blood-smeared cruel foe
He brought death, although to far too few. He gave us life once more,[103]
And from the Danes took back rich plunder. One night he stealthily
Entered the camp of the Danes, where he seized many horses.
Now, just when Heinrich began to slay these encamped marauders,
An immense clamor ascended, most like a mighty uproar—   10
Our men got no sleep, for they had to shore up the ramparts.
The Danes, as they died, let out terrible and horrendous shrieks;[104]
Our people replied with shouts—though they were shaken that once
More they had to take up the hard task of defense, as before.[105]
But too soon, Heinrich fell back from the camp of the Danes—this was
Unwise—for the Danes at once assaulted the citadel hard;
But a ruthless barrage of spears from our men met them.
Then, our warriors opened the gates and rushed forth at once.
Grim was the battle. Swords, shields clashed together ferociously.
Life cherishes my good people—it spurns those that are sinful;   20
Death cherishes the harsh foe—life plots a course for our friends;
Inhabitants find rest in sleep—the wretched are put to flight.[106]

Now, while King Siegfried and Odo were speaking to each other
Some distance from the tower, a swarm of Danes scurried forward
To capture Count Odo and carry him off with them by force.
But he struck at them first and with a mighty leap he bounded
Over the ditch below the tower, shield and spear in hand.
A hero he stood, as ever was his way, facing battle.
Then, his warriors rushed out that they might stand by their lord.[107]
His noble and doughty deeds made all those who saw him marvel.   30

Siegfried, seeing that our men were ardent in combat, said
To his followers: "Let us hurry and leave this place at once.
We can no longer stand our ground; it is best we fall back."

Ergo, suas ut Ainricus secessit ad aulas,
Germani teretis contemnunt litora sancti,
Aequivocique legunt, cuius factis bene vescor.
Circumeunt castris aequor, sed et undique vallo
Clauditur, a, dominusque meus, quasi carcere latro,
Ipse nichil peccans; murus circumdedit eius
Ecclesiam nostro celsam cogente reatu.   40
Denique rex dictus denas capiens argenti
Sex libras nitidi nobis causa redeundi
Normannis sese cunctis comitantibus, optat
Mel dulcis fluvii limfis conferre marinis,
Qualiter osque freti caudam Sequanae rapit albam
Equoreumque caput pennis quatitur Sequaninis
Ostentare; sed his autem nolentibus infit:
"Eia, Dani, muros urbis lustrate potentes;
Pergama circumquaque viri vestite valentes,
Et scapulas arcu validisque onerate sagittis.   50
Quisque ferat lapides, sed et undique tela ministret.
Hoc etiam bellum conabor et ipse videre."
Quo sermone quiescenti, surgunt simul omnes,
In que sulas penetrant, urbis sedes quibus extat,
Menia circumeunt trucibus gladiis onerati.
Digressique foras nostri circumdare turres,
Occidunt reges geminos pluresque aliorum,
Fallacesque fugam diamant verique triumphum.
Amnis in auxilium nobis Sequanae fuit altus,
Quos sorbens penitus mersit, transmisit Averno.   60
Sigemfredus ovans ridens morientibus inquit:
"Nunc vallate viri pinnas, urbem capitote,
Mensurate metris aedes, quas hic habitetis."
Inde suis: "Abeamus," ait, "tempus venit ecce,
Quo gratum fuerit nobis istinc abiisse."
Mox hilaris Sequanam liquit pro munere sumpto.
Sic alii facerent, eadem si tunc meruissent.

Quis sentire potest patula, quod subditur aure?
Terra gemat pontusque, polum latus quoque mundus:
Gozlinus, Domini praesul, mitissimus heros,   70
Astra petit Domino migrans, rutilans velut ipsa,

This occurred at the time when Heinrich returned to his own hall.[108]
They scornfully forsook the purlieus of Saint-Germain-le-Rond,[109]
And took to the field of the Saint, where I myself have life.[110]
All across this field they set up their camps, and made ramparts.
Thus, they hemmed in my blessed Master, like a thief in prison,
He who was without sin. They made a wall that encircled his
High church—indeed, such is the penalty for our great sins.[111]   40
In the end, this aforementioned king took from us pure silver,
A good sixty pounds worth, which we gave him that he might depart[112]
For his own land, and take his Norsemen with him—for he did wish
To follow the stream's honeyed course, and watch it flow to the salt
Of the sea, where the Channel seizes the white tail of the Seine,
And the river's outstretched wings cause the Ocean's head to shudder.[113]
But his men did not wish to follow him; he shouted at them:
"Fine, then, Danes. Why not go and swarm the strong walls of the city?
Mighty warriors that you are—why not besiege the ramparts,
And charge ahead, your shoulders weighed down by bows and full quivers?   50
And some can carry stones, while others bring forward javelins.
I will do what I can, as I watch you fighting fiercely."[114]
When he had finished his address, they arose and surged forward,
And made their way to the island, where the city stands.[115]
Armed with their keen-edged swords, they came and circled the ramparts.
In response, our men, then, sallied forth and ringed the tower,
And they struck down two of their kings and so many others.
The heathens took to their heels—the upright savored triumph.
And the deep, swift current of the Seine became our ally,
For it swept away and swallowed Danes; dragged them down to Hell.[116]   60
Now, Siegfried laughed and mocked those that had died and cried out to them:
"Come, brave warriors, charge the ramparts, overrun the city;
Take measure of the houses you wish to live in afterwards."[117]
Then to the men that still followed him, saying: "Let us be off,"
He said, "For the time has come for us to be gone from here."
Then, content, he left the Seine, for he had received his reward.
The others likewise might have left, had they accepted such gifts.[118]

Who shall dare to lend an ear and hear what came next?
Let the land, the sea, the sky, and all the vast, wide world lament:
Gozlin, the bishop of the Lord, and the mildest of heroes,   70
Journeyed to the Lord, sought the stars that he too might be like them.[119]

Nostra manens turris, clipeus, nec non bis-acuta
Rumphea; fortis et arcus erat fortisque sagitta.
Heu, cunctis oculos fontes terebrant lacrimarum
Atque pavore dolor contritis viscera scindit.
Tempestate sub hac Hugo princeps obit abba,
Evrardo Senones viduantur praesule docto.
Gaudia tunc hostes adipiscuntur sua laeti.
Qui vigiles madidae per opaca silentia noctis
Germanum nitida clarum vidisse figura   80
Se perhibent moetasque sui lustrasse locelli
Lumine gestantem rutilanti sepe laternam,
Quo sancti redolent artus forsan tumulati.
Instabant eius festae sollemnia lucis.
Obiurgantur et hi castellanis, quia sacra
Non celebrant; alto inde ruunt cum mente cachinno.
Mergitibus plaustrum per rura movent gravidatum,
Cuspide terga boum verso nimium stimulantes.
Protinus his propriae claudis sine crimine causae
Conectunt alios, pluresque dehinc, aliosque.   90
Certabant elegi scapulis cornuque iuvenci,
Iamque lavant proprias rubeo de sanguine costas,
Nonque valent axem terris disiungere fixum,
Attonitique stupent domni miracula nostri.
Solvuntur tauri, stimulusque ferox requievit.
Lux segetis recidiva rotas spoliis vacuavit,
Atque suis clodum revocavit motibus axem.

Effugiens horum quidam iussus iugulari,
Templa subintroiit sancti, tenuit quoque bustum
Pellitur inde miser profuga pietate necandus.   100
Vae, miseris. Multant elegum, multantur et ipsi.
Quod munus dederant socio, simili pietate
Germani meritis nactum cuncti meruerunt,
Caelitus afflicti nimium pro talibus ausis.
Unde sacerdotes statuere, locum venerantes,
Qui missas cursusque sacros illic celebrassent.
Tunc omnes cuiquam prohibent hinc tollere quicquam.
Quod violans unus proprio deferre cubili
Ecclesiae tegmen studuit; sub quo manifeste

He was our firm bulwark, our shield, our two-edged sword;
And he was our strongest bow and our keenest arrow.
Alas, fountains of tears welled up and streamed from our eyes;
Anguish sliced through our hearts that were seized by sheer terror.
During this tempest, the prince and abbot, Hugo, also died,[120]
While Sens was widowed, losing its learned prelate, Eberhard.[121]
But gladdened were our enemies and filled with immense joy.[122]
Yet, their sentries said that in the silence of the dark night,
They saw, most clearly, the bright-shining figure of Germain,   80
As he walked all about and intently surveyed his domain;
In his hand he held a lamp that gave forth a pure radiance
That shone near his redolent tomb that held his blessed limbs.[123]
When the time of his solemn feast day approached ever closer,
The inhabitants reproached the enemy that they did not
Celebrate the holy day. Then, the Danes burst out in laughter,
And went and filled a cart with sheaves and drove it across the fields,
Urging, goading the hitched oxen with the butts of their spears,
Since some of the beasts limped, not by any fault of their own;
And to grieve them further, the Danes harnessed more and more oxen.[124]   90
The poor beasts labored, struggled and strove, with horn and with haunch,
So that their straining flanks were red, awash with flowing blood—
And still they could not pull free the axle, stuck deep in the mud.
The miracles wrought by our Lord confounded the stern Danes.[125]
Then, they set free the bulls and laid aside the relentless goad.
Now, with daylight, the wheels were freed from the weight of the plunder,
And not long after, the axle came loose of its own accord.[126]

A certain Norseman, who was about to have his throat cut, fled;
Quickly he ran inside the church of the Saint, and clutched his tomb.
At once, the miserable wretch was delivered unto death.   100
Woe to such wretches: Punishing others, they too are punished,
They are given the same reward that they arranged for others,[127]
And well deserved, with equal mercy, by the grace of Germain.
Heaven condemned the evildoers for their wickedness.
Thereafter, priests were appointed to honor that holy place
By observing Holy Mass and the canonical hours;
These priests forbade the removal of anything from there.
But there was one who violated this prohibition,
And took for his bed, a coverlet from the church. But as he

Effigies eius repetita fuit puerilem;   110
Scilicet eventu nulli similante minuta,
Nota quibus fuerat pridem, nec noscitur ullo
Oppido, miror ubi venae nervique laterent,
Ossaque fugerunt pariter fugiente medulla,
Viscera speluncae tenuis foveam petiere.
Maior habebatur magnis—mirabile factum—
Is qui nunque minor pueris moriens patet esse,
Vitaque cum gemitu fugit indignata sub umbras.
Visus adest cuidam Domini sanctissimus idem
Pectore carpenti requiem per nubila noctis,   120
Marcelli sanctis precibus necnon Clodoaldi
Accipiens liquidam manibus benedicere limpham,
Unde rigans urbem, graditur per menia circum.
Huicque viro proprium promsit nomen, sed et urbi
Spem spondens, faciem liquit se conspicientem.

Nobilis hac et in urbe fuit vir carne liquescens,
Deficiens et iam flatu metuebat obire,
Castellumque capi Normannis tempore in ipso.
Attulit huic cives somnus se linquere velle,
Urbs armis quoniam cunctis deserta manebat.   130
Clericus inde venustatis mirae astitit illi,
Ore loquens placido, rutilans vultuque sereno:
"Quid metuis? Surgens tremulos depone timores,
Oblitaque fuga quamplures cerne paratos
Ad bellum." Surgens alacer muros videt omnes
Vallatos cuneis iuvenum galeis oneratum.
Voxque tonat: "Tutoribus his defenditur haec urbs;
Ast ego sum Germanus," ait, "huius quoque praesul.
Confortare, nihil formidabis, quoniam nunc
Faucibus haud sceleratorum grassabitur haec urbs."   140
Affatur sanctus, redamatque virum caro, flatus;
Affatur felix, fugitque virum mala pestis;
Alloquitur sanctus; lecto surrexit egrotus;
Almis faminibus sospes procedit egrotus;
Explicuit, visu noctis quod noverat ipse.
Luce dehinc quadam dum gestabatur et almi
Militibus propriis corpus per moenia circum.

Lay beneath it, his body became that of a little lad—   110
It dwindled so much – such a thing has never before been seen:
He who was once known to all, could now be recognized by none.
Who can say what became of his arteries and all his thews,
Or how his bones and his marrow could entirely vanish,
Or how his entrails could fit inside such a small, narrow gut.
He who was judged taller than the tallest—a true miracle—
Now, in death, became not much bigger than a small, little lad:
With a great groan, his wretched life fled to dwell among the shades.[128]
Then, this same and most holy Saint of the Lord next appeared
To an inhabitant, sound asleep in the deep of the night—   120
The pleas of the blessed Marcellus and Clodoald sent him.[129]
He took in his hands lustral water, which is used in blessings,
And sprinkled it on the city, walking along the ramparts.
He then revealed his name to this man, and gave to the city
His promise of hope. Then, he faded from the sight of this man.

A certain nobleman of the city, whose flesh had withered,
Believed he was going to die, for his breath was growing weak;
He thought the fortifications were overrun by Norsemen.
Then, in a dream, he saw the citizens leaving him behind,
Because the city was completely bereft of warriors.[130]   130
Then he saw, standing by his bedside, a priest of great beauty,
Who spoke most sweetly and whose face radiated serenely:
"Why are you fearful? Rise up. Put aside dread, tremble not.
Behold, the warriors have not fled, but have taken up arms
For battle." Then that nobleman arose and saw the ramparts
All bristling with countless young men, each one girt in his bright helm.
And a voice was heard: "Here are warriors to ward the city;
And as for me," he said, "I am Germain, this city's bishop.
Now be of good courage; fear not, because from this day forth
This city shall not fall prey to the jaws of these ravishers."[131]   140
Thus spoke the Saint. Breath returned to this nobleman; his flesh healed–
The blessed one spoke; the foul pestilence fled from this man;
The holy one spoke—the sick nobleman arose from his bed.[132]
Saved by these words of life, this nobleman walked off fully healed
And told of what he had seen during the night in a vision.
One day, as the Saint's blessed body was being carried in
Solemn procession to the many parts of the city wall

Urbanis septum sectantibus, omnipotentem
Perrogitando Deum votis sub voce canora,
Caeditur allofilo de portatoribus unus   150
Nomine Gozbertus calclo; percussor in umbras
Tartareas fugit moriens, icto patiente
Nil super hoc lapidis iactu, sancto auxiliante.
Interea caedis validae corrupta procellis
Urbs patitur gladium exterius, loeti quoque pestis,
Eheu, nobilium plebes penitus laniabat.
Interius nec erat nobis tellus, obeuntum
Quae praebere sepulturam membris potuisset
Comminus; ulla dies nec erat, quae non generasset
Urbanos interque suburbanos truculentos   160
Bella, nec ulla abiit prope, quae non interfectos
Pestiferos secum duxisset ad antra gehennae.

Rex igitur venturus Odo transmittitur inde
Francorum Karolo suprafato basileo,
Quatinus auxilio caeleri succurreret urbi.
Post nullus procerum remanet nisi Marcius abba,
Sepe supra cuius memoratio scripta relucet.
Ipse equites ex more Danum vestire coegit
Sex solos, redeunte die quadam, super arva,
Transque volant illi Sequanam camposque peragrant   170
Ex variis plenos armis sevoque sopore,
Normannosque necant totidem fuerant quot et ipsi.
Nascitur hinc strepitus castris; horum resonante
Voce, truces carpunt clipeos nostrique carinam.
Nostra Dionisii tondebant littora sancti
Pecora, quae duxere sibi crebro speculata.
Verum illis Ebolus iugiter fuit obvius abba,
Qui quorum comitem quadam stravit vice telo.
Unde Dani linquunt ripam, referuntque cadaver.
Mox Ebolus senos equites dimisit ab arce,   180
Quattuor hi ternosque necant certamine diro.
Nocte quidem cives crebrius pecorum sub opaca
Custodes adeunt, quosdamque fugant, aliosque
Attribuunt iugulis, hoc egeruntque frequenter,
Indicioque tulere Danos urbi sine flatu

By his followers and many of the inhabitants, who
Loudly besought Almighty God in a chorus of voices,
One of the bearers, whose name was Gosbert, was struck by a   150
Stone cast by a pagan. And yet it was the thrower that fell
Down dead; his soul fled into the shades of Tartarus—and he
That was hit by the stone stood unscathed, protected by the Saint.
Now all this while, the wearied city, struck low by the frightful
Onslaught of carnage, suffered the sword without, the plague within.
Alas, so greatly were the ranks of the noblemen thinned out
That our hands could provide no fitting place of burial
Which could serve as sepulchers for all the bodies of the dead.
Not a single day went by when there was not stirred up strife
Between the inhabitants and the grim foe beyond the walls.   160
Not a single day went by that did not see one of our
Men, though struck to death, also send a Dane far down to dark Hell.

Afterwards, Odo, the future king, was sent from the city
To Charles, the Emperor of the Franks, of whom we have spoken,
To ask him to come swiftly and bring succor to the city.[133]
After Odo, no lord remained, except that warlike abbot,
Whose great and shining deeds I have often mentioned already.[134]
When light again traversed across the meadows, he commanded
That just six horsemen array themselves in the manner of Danes.
These six promptly crossed over the Seine and rode across the fields,   170
Where grim weapons and the sleep of the dead were to be found.
They fell upon the Norsemen and killed as many as themselves.
A clamor arose in the Danish camp; screams, shouts resounded.
The grim foes seized their bucklers, while our men took the ship.
Now, our herds often grazed by the banks near Saint Dénis,
And the Norsemen, who saw them, frequently made off with many.
But Abbot Ebolus always cut them off on the way back.
One time, with his spear, he killed one of their high chieftains—
The Danes had to abandon the banks and carry off the corpse.
Next, Ebolus sent horsemen from the tower, six in number,   180
Who engaged in a hard fight and slew four times three of the foe.
Many times, certain inhabitants, in the dark of night, would
Go and attack those that guarded the herds, putting some to flight,
And slaying the rest. They carried out these exploits quite often.
To prove their success, they brought back to the city dead Danes,

Atque simul vivos, ut sic credi potuissent.
In que sulam penetrant solito quadam vice ritu,
Maenia qua resident urbis, saevi trecenti.
Protinus ense quium bino stravere novenos,
Vulnera deposuere quibus triginta. Nec extat   190
Posse datum quarti lumen spectare diei.
Congressi nostrum gemini, qui morte fruentes
Egregia sanctos vexere pedes super astra;
Nam senior Segebertus erat, iunior Segevertus.

Forte deinde, tribus cuneis cinctus galearum,
Armipotens montis super Odo cacumina Martis
Enituit, cuius clipeos novus inradiavit
Sol, croceo Oceani thalamo vastipede spreto.
Hunc prius Elios adamans quam rura salutat.
Quem visu capiunt cives et amore sub alto.   200
Ast hostes, prohibere fores turris cupientes,
Transsiliunt Sequanam, vallantes littora circum.
Reddidit Odo tamen castellanis equitando
Se medios inter sevos, Ebolo reserante
Huic portas, cunctique stupent hoc nobile factum.
Hinc eius socios retro statim redeuntes
Ferreus insequitur hostis, post terga meando.
Plus geminis etiam leugis; interfuit illis
Dictus Adalaelmus superis pridem comes; idem:
"Eia," suis inquit, "satius pergamus in illos,   210
Quam nos hic illi inveniant." Adalaelmus hoc inquit.
Pestiferi petiere fugam, nostrique tropheum.
Scuta tonant, dardique volant, et corpora Danum
Consulis arva tegunt gladio regnante Adalaelmi.
Non dimisit eos, donec repedare coegit
Ad fluvium, posthac et ovans victorque reversus.
En et Ainricus, superis crebro vocitatus,
Obsidione volens illos vallare, necatur.
Inque suos, nitens Sequanam transire, Danorum
Rex Sinric, geminis ratibus spretis, penetravit   220
Cum sociis ternam quinquagenis, patiturque
Naufragium medio fluvii fundum petiturus,
Quo fixit, comitesque simul, tentoria morti.

And some that were still alive—to lend credence to their tales.[135]
One time, three hundred ferocious Danes came on to the island,[136]
As was their wont, hard by that place where the walls were low.[137]
But without delay, two of our men met them, swords in hand,
And they struck down nine times thirty of the enemy, meting   190
Out deadly strokes—no Dane there saw the light of the fourth day.
Then, these twins of ours met a great and honorable death,
In this way, they set their feet on the path above the stars:
The eldest was called Segebert and the younger Segevert.[138]

Then, the noble warrior, Odo, with three battalions,
All girt in shining helms, was seen on the heights of Montmartre.[139]
The shafts of the sparkling sun, newly risen from the golden
Couch of the ocean, made their bright bucklers glimmer and glint.
Helios prized this hero, and hailed him first, then touched the fields.[140]
The inhabitants, too, beheld him, whom they greatly adored.   200
The Danes sought to deny him the approach to the tower gates;
So they crossed the Seine and took up positions along the banks.
However, Odo turned towards the city and galloped hard
Right through the throngs of the harsh foe—all the while, Ebolus held
Open the gates for him. Everyone marveled at this bold deed.
Then his companions at once followed the very same course,
While the iron-hard enemy fiercely chased after them
For a distance of some two leagues. Among these companions[141]
Was Adalhelm the count, of whom we have spoken already.[142]
"Come," he told his men, "it is better that we turn and face them,   210
Rather than have them run up behind us." Thus spoke Adalhelm.
Then, the cruel Danes were put to flight, and our men triumphed.
Shields were pounded and arrows flew, and the corpses of the Danes
Littered the fields, struck down by the noble sword of Adalhelm.
He did not let up—not until he drove them right back to the
River. Only then did he turn away in joyful triumph.
And behold, at that time, Heinrich, mentioned already, was killed,
As he was trying to besiege the camp of the enemy.[143]
Now, one of the kings of the Danes, Sinric, sought to cross the Seine
To get to his men. He spurned two of the boats that were readied   220
For him, and boarded a third instead, along with fifty men.
Midstream, the boat keeled over, and down to the bottom they went—
He and his men set up their tents in the realm of the dead.[144]

Hic sua castra prius Sequanae contingere fundum
Quo surgens oritur dixit quam linquere regnum
Francorum; fecit Domino tribuente, quod inquit.

Denique, cum medius Titane incenditur orbis,
Cumque sitit tellus pecorique libet magis umbra,
Sibilat et gratus silvas zephyrus per amenas,
Pergama loetiferis stipantur ab hostibus urbis,　　　　　　　　230
Quae passim patiebatur certamen; et unum
Bellabant muri, speculae, pontes quoque cuncti,
Pugnabat pelagus, contra tellus magis ampla.
Classica valde tonant, mensis discedere cives.
"Eus," clamant litui, "convivia temnite cuncti."
Urbs terrore, simul cives, invaditur omnis.
Nullus in urbe locus fuerat, qui bella lateret.
Pila falas, laceraeque tegunt nimium catapultae
Arva velut pluviae, plumbi nec non onerosi
Poma dabant peltis gemitus et grandia saxa.　　　　　　　　240
Haec nobis illi tribuebant praemia semper.
At contra lapides rapidos pariterque balistas
Direxere feris nostri celeresque sagittas.
His aer seritur hinc inde volantibus amplum.
Non inter caelos aliud tranabat et arva.
Mars magis atque magis regnat tumidusque superbit.
Virgo Dei Genovefa caput defertur ad urbis,
Quo statim meritis eius nostri superarunt;
Inde fugaverunt etiam pinnis procul illos.
Robore qui multus fuerat, sed corpore parvus,　　　　　　　　250
Gesserit hoc miles quinis comitatus ab armis,
Gerboldus, nusquam cuius petiit catapultae
Sanguinei rostrum siccam sine fluminis unda.
Partibus ex aliis longe surgunt acriora
Praelia; plangores clipeique cient galeaeque
Stridores. Nostri bellant, sed fortius illi.
Defecere fatigati beno quoque dextri.

Pro dolor, alta nimis flentes lamenta trahebant.
Cana senecta gemit multum florensque iuventa.
Plorabant monachi, lacrimatur clericus omnis,　　　　　　　　260

He had boasted that he would rather camp on the very bed
Of the Seine, even if he had to go its source, than leave
The kingdom of France. And, indeed, the Lord let him keep his word.[145]

As Titan, in the middle of its course, set alight the world,
So the earth thirsted and the herds sought the good comfort of shade,
Though soothing Zephyrus blew sweetly through the charming forests,
The mortal enemies of the city encircled its walls,   230
So that it had to face constant attacks from all directions.
On the walls, the towers, and all the bridges battle was joined;
Even the waves took up the fight, as did the expansive land.
Loud were the horns, urging inhabitants to leave their tables.
"Arise," cried out the horns, "let everyone forsake his repast."[146]
Terror enveloped the city and all its inhabitants.
There was no place in the city free from fierce battle.
Spears, missiles hurled by the catapults shrouded the towers,
And fell like rain upon the fields. Great balls of lead, hardly light,
And large stones crashed and thudded into bucklers, making them groan.   240
Such were the constant rewards that the enemy gave to us.
And in reply, our men shot back at the harsh enemy—
Rocks and projectiles and arrows—and all of them swift and true.
Here and there, the air was woven thick with missiles;
Nothing else could be seen flying between the fields and the sky.
The reign of Mars grew vaster and vaster and he filled with pride.[147]
God's virgin, Geneviève, was then brought before the city.[148]
And then, by the merit of her grace, our men were favored,
And they put the enemy to flight; chased the Danes from the walls.
The warrior who did this deed, helped by five companions,   250
Was certainly short in stature but filled with valiant strength—
Gerbold was he called—and never did his arrows fall to earth[149]
Without wounding and causing to flow currents of rushing blood.
In other parts of the city, the battle grew most bitter—
Bucklers thudded and sorely resounded, while helmets loudly
Clanged. Hard fought our men, but the enemy proved far stronger.
Greatly wearied by battle the strength of the righteous was sapped.[150]

Ah, how doleful were the tears, groans; how ceaseless the mourning
Made by the white-haired old men and those in the flower of
Their youth; the monks also wept, as did all of the clergy.   260

Aera voce tonant, luctus sed et aethra facessit.
Hi tristes animos urbem metuendo revelant
Hoste capi; caelo laeti torquere cachinnos
Moenia vocisonos rentes lucrare, severi,
Femineusque iubas sexus lugens lacerando,
Verrebat terras proprio de crine soluto.
Eheu, nuda suis quatiebant pectora pugnis,
Un que gulis facies secuerunt, tristia ac ora.
Voce rogant lacrimosa omnes: "Germane beate,
Auxiliare tuis, alioquin nunc moriemur.   270
O pie, nunc succurre citus, succurre perimus."
Germanum reboat tellus; necnon fluviusque,
Littora et omne nemus pariter circum resonabat.
"O Germane sacer, nobis miserere, rogamus."
Templorum campana boant merentia, clamant,
Vocibus his et humus tremuit flumenque remugit.
Urbs extrema verens instantis carpere lucis
Omnia lamentis lacrimans spargebat amaris.
Omnibus en Germanus adest recolendus in orbe,
Corpore subsidioque simul nil, vota moratus,   280
Quo maiora tenebantur certamina Martis,
Signiferosque Danum lucrari morte coegit,
Atque dehinc alios perplures, protenus urbe,
Ponte simul, pellens illos; quem maxima turris
Ante suos domnum speculans congaudet ocellos.
Unde fatigati vires revocant sibi fortes
Atque resistere decertant bellando protervis,
Qui turrim repetunt, pontem vel menia linquunt.
Mille simul speculae stabant, omnes quia pugnae
Multo non una poterant numero prohibente.   290
Dilabuntur humi vario traiecta mucrone
Viscera, quo pluvie celo, ratibusque feruntur.

Iam capiente iubar migrans sub marmora Tetis
Oceano, foribus turris submittitur altus
Valde focus. Flammae praecelsa cacumina turris
Cingebant, armis pugnant ignique sinistri
Linquitur arcs dextris, valvasque iubent aperire,
Optantes prorsus preciosam scandere mortem

Moans charged the air; the ethereal vault filled with dirges.
Fear imbued our hearts—the Danes might capture the city—
While joyful howls and shrieks from these cruel ones rose to the sky;
For, indeed, they thought themselves masters of the walls already.
The female sex sobbed in anguish; women tore their hair;
Their tresses, which now were hanging free, swept upon the ground.
Alas, they then bared their breasts; beat them with their fists.
With their nails they tore at their faces, twisted with grief.[151]
With voices soaked in tears, each one cried out: "Blessed Germain,
Come to the aid of your people so that we may not perish.   270
O holy Saint, save us, help us swiftly that we may not die."
All the land and the river rang out with the name of Germain;
The banks and all the surrounding forests echoed together:
"O holy Germain, have mercy upon us, thus do we pray."
And then the church bells let loose their mournful, grief-stricken peals,
At the sound of which the earth trembled and the river did moan,
And the dawn was seen as an omen of doom by the city—
Bitter were the tears, the lamentations that then arose.
Then behold—Germain, worthy of praise by the world, showed himself
In body, to bring aid, in answer to our pleas. He showed   280
Himself on the field of Mars, where hardest raged the battle,
Drove the standard-bearers of the Danes into death's embrace,
Along with many more. Thus, he forced them back from the city
As well as the bridge. And then, those in the high tower looked out
At the Lord of the city—and seeing him, their eyes were[152]
Filled with joy. Our men, though wearied, recovered their strength,
Took heart, and began to fight the grim foe with greater resolve,
So that the Danes ceased attacking the walls and the bridge, and stormed
The tower. A thousand of them hung back and watched—not all could
Join in the fight together, so densely did they press forward.   290
Many that had climbed up fell to the ground like rain from the sky,
Their entrails gushing out, slashed by swords; ships bore them away.

Now, when the sun sank down to the marble palace of Thetis,[153]
In the depths of the ocean, the Danes heaped a pile of wood
In front of the tower—the flames began to eddy upwards—
In this way, the vile Norsemen fought with iron and fire.
The righteous abandoned the tower and opened the gates;
It was more preferable to them to face glorious death,

Plus quam fallacum fidei committere semet.
Nemo stetit supra speculam, solus nisi sepe   300
Iam sancti famulus dicti lignum Crucis almae
In flammas retinens, oculis haec vidit et inquit;
Densus enim fumus nimium velaverat illam.
Tum, portis igitur reseratis, aridus ense
Portuni madido moritur Vulcanus inermis,
Subtilemque fugam petiere cadavera torvi
Multa reportantes secum, Mavorsque quievit.
Haec virtute Crucis sanctae victoria nostris
Caeditur et meritis Germani antistitis almi,
Quem reveunt ad bassilicam Stephani quoque testis   310
Gaudentes populi praecelsa: "Te," reboantes
Voce. "Deum, te laudamus dominumque fatemur."
Urbis erat praesul clarus, tutamen et urbis,
Mesticiam alterutrim nactae sic letitiamque.

Funditus his animo versus tamquam mare choro,
"Cernere," Francigenos[4] inquit, "properate sub urbem
Sexcentis statum nostris suggestibus aptum.
Talia me coram fures?" Iussis opus addunt.
Dum tamen hos trames revehit primatis ad aulam,
Sectantur, glomerant cuneos posterga nefandi,   320
Committunt, superant, cedunt, fugiunt, moriuntur.
Templa fugax coetus penetrat confinia muris.
Victorum gemini quandam—mirabile narro—
Ecclesiam inrumpunt, farsam de morte relinquunt.
Post et equos saltu repetunt paribusque coherent.
Sic ternis Sequanam Martisque cacumina stratis
Sexcenti copulant ex milibus, hinc remeantque;
Namque triumphantes fratrum promsit geminorum
Fama fuisse Teoderici procerum ast Aledramni.

En princeps de quo canitur, circumdatus armis   330
Omnigenis, caelum veluti splendoribus astreis,
Induperator adest Karolus comitatus opimo

---

[4] An alternative reading in A. GP, PW, and HW suggest *Francigenis*.

Rather than place their trust in these godless, deceitful men.
Only one man remained, then, on the tower, all by himself;   300
He served the Saint mentioned already, and held high a wooden
Cross out towards the flames; he told later what his eyes beheld:
A dense smoke had begun to circle all around the tower;
The gates then opened, and by the wetted sword of Portunus,[154]
Vulcan, deprived of his hot and dry weapons, was forthwith slain.
Then, the wretched Danes fell back; took to flight, taking with them
A great many of the corpses; and only then did Mars rest.
Through the power and strength of this holy cross alone did we
Gain victory, and by the great virtues of Bishop Germain.
They brought back the Saint inside the Basilica of Stephen,[155]   310
And the people let forth shouts. "Thou," their loud voices rang out,
"We praise, as we do God, for thou art indeed our master."
He was the famous bishop of the city, and its keeper—
A city that had passed in turn from lamentation to joy.[156]

These events much moved Charles, like as the sea is moved by the wind,
And he spoke to six hundred Franks: "Go, search out the approaches
To the city, where we might best establish our camp.
How dare these brigands act thus, before my very face?" Then,
The Franks did as he bid; their path led to the bishop's hall.[157]
But the pagan warriors swiftly regrouped; chased close behind.   320
The battle was joined. They were crushed. They yielded, fled and were killed.
Fleeing Danes broke into the churches that stood near the walls.[158]
Two of our conquering men—marvelous to relate—burst
Into one church—left it only when it was stuffed with the dead;
Then, they leaped on horses, rode back to their companions.
These six hundred Franks linked together the Seine with Montmartre
By so many rows of the dead—some three thousand Danes were slain.
Fame has it that these two most valorous and young noble men
Were also brothers, whose names were Theodric and Aledram.[159]

The prince, for whom this song is sung, then appeared, surrounded   330
By arms of all sort, just as the sky is filled with splendid stars.
This was Charles, the high Emperor, who was attended by his

Diversi populo labii, tentoria figens
Sub Martis pedibus montis, speculamque secundum.
Redditur ecclesiaeque diu pastor viduatae
Nobilis egregiusque sacrae pompatus honore
Totius Anschericus virtutis, germine clarus.
Annuiturque feris licitum Senones adeundi,
Septies argenti libris causa redeundi
Martis mense datis centum sua ad impia regna.   340
Tunc glaciabantur torpentis saecla Novembris.
Sic Karolus rediit, moriturus fine propinquo.

Nomina, tunc ensem quorum perpessa fuisti,
Nec vocitabas[5] prius, pigra, O Burgundia bello,
Nustria praecluibus thalamum nisi comeret altis
Iam tibi consilio facilis; verum modo iam scis.

Inde revertentes prato sua castra reponunt
Iam dicto, templum sancti velut ante colentes.
Quattuor hic dominusque mei Germanus in usum
Contractos nimium membris priscum revocavit,   350
Motibus atque suis admoverat organa fibris,
Subducto genibus dudum pedibusque parato
Iure suo, extinctisque fenestris unius orbi
Restituit radios solis spectare micantes.
Beisino huc adiens inter saevos comitatu
Laesa nihil quodam, meritis sed tuta beati
Femina, post quaedam meruit lumen quoque caeca.
Cuius ad accubitat puteus vestigia, cuius
Qui potabit aquas, extemplo febre laborans,
Auxilio sancti fidens capiet medicinam.   360
His panem cupiens quaedam componere, iussit
Vi sibi scorta[6] Danum deferri; namque sacerdos

---

[5] An emendation for *vocitare* in A, which GP, PW, and HW retain.
[6] An emendation for *scotta* in A, which GP, PW, and HW retain. Female camp-followers were *de rigueur* during this time, and given the obvious authority with which she demands water, it is not possible that she is a slave of any sort, as suggested by Adams and Riggs in their translation (p. 54, n. 162).

Band of retainers, diverse men, of varied tongues, who set up
Their tents at the foot of Montmartre, near the tower.[160]
Then, the long-widowed congregation was again given a
Pastor: this glorious honor of great renown now fell to
The illustrious Anscheric, in whom virtues brightly shone.[161]
Then, the heathens were permitted to make their way to Sens
And were given seven hundred silver pounds on the promise
That come March, they would all return to their accursed kingdoms.[162]   340
This happened when the world was benumbed by icy November.
Charles, then, went away; it was not long afterwards that he died.[163]

You could not know about these heathens whose swords were to bring you
Much grief, O Burgundy, little accustomed to war, had not
Neustria led her highborn daughters to the conjugal bed.
Heed well this counsel—for now you too know who these heathens are.[164]

In the year 887.
The Danes returned from Burgundy, and set up camp in the fields[165]
As before, and rendered the same rough homage to the Saint's church.
At this time, my Lord Germain cured four men, who were halt and lame,[166]
And made them vigorous once more, as they had been long before,   350
Loosening the sinews and thews; bracing them to stir and move—
The usage their knees and feet formerly had known was restored.
To another, the windows of whose eyes were shut and darkened,
He gave sight, so that the bright-shining beams of the sun burst through.
A woman came from Bessin, and though she traversed through the armed
Heathen camp, she was unharmed, by virtue of the Saint's power;
Indeed, blind she was and later was given the gift of sight.
There lies, at the steps of Germain's church, a well. Those that drink[167]
Of its efficacious waters, with great and resolute faith—
Though they be wracked with fevers—are straightaway restored to health.   360
There was a certain harlot of the Danes who wished to bake bread.
She sent for this water, to be brought by force or bought—for a

Templa tuens, puteum vendebat egris precio amplo.
Depositus flammae panis mox ipse figuram
Sanguinis accepit rubeam. Post altera forte
Scitur vi conans latices hausisse cruorem.

Quis tanti peragrare potest miracula sancti?
Ora mihi si mille aderant, totidem quoque linguae
Vocibus explentes aer caelumque boatu,
Gesta mei narrare patris numerumve nequissem.   370
Hic Germanus, hic est, qui passus adhuc renitere
Haud mundo, cunctis nimiumque stupenda peraegit,
Fundere signa prius didicit genetricis in alvo,
Anteque virtutem celsam quam cernere lucem.
Talia quis, lector, sanctorum gesserit umquam?
Caedo, sacer forsan, sodes, babtista Iohannes.
Ergo, meus similis Germanus huic habeatur.
Iste cadaveribus ternis vitam revocavit,
Restituens lapsis proprias sedes animabus.

Urbs age Parisius, sub quis defensa fuisti   380
Principibus? "Me quis poterat defendere, primas
Hic nisi Germanus, virtus et amor meus omnis?
Post regem regum sanctamque eius genetricem
Rex meus ipse fuit pastorque, comes quoque fortis;
Hic ensis bisacutus adest meus, is catapulta,
Is clipeusque, patens murus, velox sed et arcus."
His quia sat silvae resonant Filomela quiescat.

Plectra revolvamus vocis post terga stuporum.
Foedere quo fragili fuerant infecta, loquamur,
Agmina Normannum Francis e finibus antra   390
Ad sua nolentum descendere, sed Sequanina
Immo fluenta cupiscentum tua rursus adire,
Quae, argentum sibimet retinendo novalia monstrent,
O Burgundia. Non; simulata cupido latebat;
Quod sequitur, cordi affuerat, sed hoc tamen ori.
Concipiunt igitur Thetis nitendo quadrigas
Munere clam gratum pontes transcendere iusto.
Ilicet Anscherici defertur episcopi ad escas

Priest, the church's warden, sold it to the sick at a high price.[168]
Now, when she placed the bread into the flames to bake, it took on
The red color and hue of blood. Then, another harlot sought
To drink some of this water, and as is known, drew only blood.[169]

How can the miracles of this Saint be fully recounted?
Had I a thousand mouths and the same number of tongues as well,[170]
Which could fill the air, the heavens with their cries and shouts,
Still I could not narrate all the deeds of my saintly father.[171]   370
Such is Germain. Indeed, though he can no more be seen shining
In the world, yet the deeds he accomplished did astonish all.
While still in his mother's womb, he gave forth the very first signs
Of his great virtues, even before he saw the light of day.[172]
Is there another, O reader, who has done such saintly deeds?
Perhaps John the Baptist was one such holy man, if you will—
Therefore, my beloved Germain should likewise be adored,
Who also caused life to return into three cadavers, and
By doing so, restored to these three souls their due abodes.[173]

O Paris, say, which among the princes rose to your defense?[174]   380
"Who, indeed, could protect me first and foremost, if it were not
This very Germain, who is my might, to whom I give my love?
After the King of kings, Beloved of His holy Mother,
There can be but one king for me, my shepherd, my stalwart count.
He is ever my double-edged sword, my mighty catapult,
My hard-wearing shield, my encircling wall, my supple bow."[175]
The woods rang with the people's songs; Philomela fell silent.[176]

With these miracles told, let us once again tune the lyre.
Let us then speak of the fragile accord struck with the Norsemen,   390
Who left not France for their caves, but sought passage to the Seine,[177]
For they yearned to overrun your fields, O Burgundy—they, who
Took the silver, and then did other than what they had promised.[178]
It was all a ruse, for they kept their greed deeply hidden,
So what was in their hearts was not the same as what was on
Their lips. Thus, they made a plan to ram hard at the bridges
With the chariots of Thetis, and thus get clear of them.[179]
Now, Bishop Anscheric heard the ensuing tumult, for he

Ast Eboli[7]—ferclis inerant Titane secante
Lucifluam cernente poli gnomone figuram—   400
Multiplici remo contundere pocula limfae.
Scandere gentiles undas conclamat eoas
Parisius; surgit securus uterque ciborum,
Arma ciunt ripasque legunt pinnasque facessunt.
Hic Ebolus[8] raptat cordam vibratque sagittam.
Quam nauclerus in ascellam per navis iatum
Praevius accepit modicum terebroque foratum.
Sic auriga necis casus pelagique faselus
Quin patitur. Restant igitur caeduntque sub arcem
Acephali; quoniam Christum perdunt, caput ipsum.   410

At vero veniam deposcunt, obsidibusque
Iusiuranda parant aliud non tangere litus
Ni Sequanae gressumque referre cito velut ante.
Nam nobis dederant tranquillum Matrona flumen
Quidquid alit, solito securum quod vocitamus.
Hoc nostris violare Danos ingens erat horror.
Unde forum foedus pariter commune fiebat,
Una domus, panis, potus, sedes, via, lectus,
Commixtum sibimet populum mirantur utrumque.
Quod pactum Senones primum statuere migrando   420
Hactenus et servaverunt, quoad usque secundo
Menibus invitis superos latices adipisci
Fas meruere; dato barcas per flumina raptant.
Eheu, catholicos secum per littora vitae
Bisdenos siquidem aut necibus lorisve plicarunt.
Mox adhibent propriis vitam sine mandere castris
Vallatam geminis mortem sine tegmine prunas;
Quae nostri praecibus sperarunt tuta tenere.
Securum frangunt, Senones tempnunt Matronamque
Aequoreo curru sulcant. Mandatur et urbi.   430
Guttura millenis crepitant, planctu quoque, bombis.
Pax communis abit, foedus pessumdatur omne.
Continuo cuncti torvos disquirere cives

---

[7] A reads *Ebali*, as do GP, PW, and HW.
[8] *Ebalus* in A and retained in GP, PW, and HW.

Was at repast with Ebolus—it was at that time of day
When the light of Titan cut in half the sky's luminous face—[180]   400
They heard the heathens thrashing the river, to its depths, with oars.
"They are gaining the current from the East!" Thus did all Paris
Cry out. The two at once arose; they cared no more for food.
They called for arms, for the banks to be secured, the walls shored up.
Ebolus seized a bow, drew back the cord, let an arrow fly.
It shot right through the open oar-hole on the flank of the ship
That was leading the charge, and struck the pilot in the armpit.
Thus died the leader of the fleet; his sea-chariot went down;
The rest resisted; then yielded beneath the walls. These Danes are
Headless men, indeed, for they know not Christ, the Head of us all.[181]   410

Thereupon, the Norsemen sued for peace; offered hostages,
And swore an oath that they would land on no other shore than that
Of the Seine and would fall back to their prior positions.
And as for the region nourished by the Marne, they would leave it
In peace, for which they gave us "full assurance," as it is called.[182]
But we feared that the Danes would not stand by this assurance;
And yet, because of it, both us and they, abided in peace—
We both began to share the same house, bread, drink, seat, road, bed.
Both our people marveled that we could mingle easily.[183]
This kind of pact was first established in the region of Sens.[184]   420
They kept the bargain until they were freely allowed to drag
Their ships, despite our walls, to the upper current. Once
Gained, they swiftly floated their vessels on the river's flow.
Alas, they also dragged off with them, along the shore, Christians,
Twenty in all, yet alive—bound for the sword, or bondage, and
Soon to endure life in their camps—without food—death behind
Double ditches, like coals that no one wants to cover and keep.[185]
But they remained safe in their camps, helped by our prayers.
The Danes broke the oath, scorned Sens, and led their sea-chariots
To the waters of the Marne. The city, then, heard the tidings.[186]   430
A thousand throats broke out in bitter cries and lamentations.
Dead was the shared peace, gone the accord of the assurance.
Swiftly, the inhabitants ran throughout the city and the

Urbe, foro currunt, aliqui si forte paterent.
Evax, inveniunt quingen, plagisque trucidant.
His micuit praestans Ebolus Mavortius abba,
Ni cupidus nimium lascivus, ne omnibus aptus.
Nam pulchre nituit studiis quae gramma ministrat.
Foederis antistes causa permisit abire
Anschericus tentos, potius concidere debens. 440
Inde feri Meldis feriunt, urbem quoque vallant.

Interea Karolus regno vita quoque nudus,
Viscera Opis divae conplectitur abdita tristis.
Laetus Odo regis nomen regni quoque numen,
Francorum populo gratante faventeque multo
Ilicet, atque manus sceptrum, diademaque vertex.
Francia laetatur, quamvis is Nustricus esset;
Nam nullum similem sibimet genitum reperire.
Nec quia dux illi Burgundia defuit; eius
Nustria ad insignis nati concurrit honorem. 450
Sic uno ternum congaudet ovamine regnum.
Praeterea astutos petiit praeceps Aquitanos.
Mox sibi subiectis Francorum regna revisit,
Moenia Meldis adhuc Danis stipantibus urbis,
Cui praesul fuerat residens in ea Segemundus,
Preasulis Anscherici Tetbertus belliger heros,
Germanus consul. Minime Delius neque Febe
Apportabat ei spatium, iuge sed sibi bellum
Undique constat, eisque tamen per multa resistit.
Perdidit innumeros, quotiens ex agmine saevo 460
Exiliens, citra muros pessumdare tetros.
Flamina quot tulerat telis, orare nequibo.
Pro dolor. Armipotens inter mortalia defit
Arma ruens, nunquam sibi principe subveniente,
Exitiumque polis posthac cum praesule capto
Passa luit; regi hinc felix micat omen Odoni.

Denique Luteciae revolant ad culmina tutae.
Convocat huc omnes proprios per regna morantes;

Marketplaces, seeking cruel heathens, if they could be found.
Happily, they found some fifty, and struck them down and slew them.[187]
In this feat, Ebolus, that fighting abbot, did brightly shine;
If not for his greed and lewdness, he was fit for all exploits,[188]
Since he was renowned for his knowledge in letters and grammar.
Because Bishop Anscheric wished to adhere to the treaty,
He let some of the captives go free; he could have killed them all.[189]   440
Then, these same cruel heathens struck at Meaux, laying siege to it.

In the year 888.
During this time, Charles, stripped of his life and also his kingdom,
Filled with great sadness, sought out the eternal dark depths of Ops.[190]
Gladly Odo took the title and authority of king;
He was happily supported by all the Frankish people;
In his hand was placed the scepter; on his head was placed the crown.[191]
France was filled with joyfulness, although he came from Neustria;[192]
Never would she find another like him, among her children.
Nor did Burgundy, which had a duke no less worthy, hold back[193]
To give honor to this illustrious son of Neustria.   450
Thus did the three parts of the realm unite in joyous triumph.[194]
But first of all, Odo swiftly marched against sly Aquitaine;[195]
Once he had subjected them, he returned to his realm of France,
Where the Danes were yet encircled around the walls of Meaux,[196]
In which the good bishop, Sigemund, was still in residence,
Along with that stout warrior and brother to Anscheric,
That is, Count Tetbert, whom neither Delos nor Phoebus granted
A moment's respite—forever was he beset by constant
Grim battles, and ever did he firmly resist and fight back.[197]
A great number he slew from among the gathered host of foes,   460
When he leaped over the walls and attacked the cruel heathens.
How many were the souls his arrows wrenched away, cannot be
Told. But, alas, when this warrior, strong in battle, headlong
Rushed into mortal combat, he was struck down, for no leader
Came to his aid. The city was ruined; its bishop captured.
But this was a most fortuitous warning for King Odo.[198]

In the year 889.
Then the Danes sought again the high, safe walls of Lutetia,
Where Odo had summoned the men of his realms who served him;

En sine iam numero numerum praestans Odo nectit.
Francigeni approperant alta cum fronte superbi.   470
Calliditate venis acieque, Aquitania, linguae,
Consilioque fugae Burgun—adiere—diones.
Sessio fit non longa satis frustrata triumpho.
Nescio quis socios lusit Danosque cecidit
Non paucos, modico quamvis, ut fama, popello,
Quo ventus veniens, Ademarus nomine dictus.
Sclademarusque dehinc binos iugulis dedit, isque
Deditus est idem primus; primum duit umbris
Luteciae torvum, postquam primo patuere.
Principium gladii tenuit finemque recepit,   480
Hoc super infidos, illum corpus super eius.
Rotberti fuerat pugnax comitis Sclademarus.
Dispulerat galeas terror propriumque sub urbem
Lunatas stadiis libitum peltas trecentis.
Praeterea quadringentis a mille remotis
Acefalos prostravit humi peditum comitatus
Agmine tercentum pastor certamine acerbo
Nobilis Anschericus, pollens ex virginis ore.
Sic alacres spolium revehunt ad moenia multum
Urbani praestante Deo qui regnat ab alto.   490

Expediamus abhinc dignos Odone triumphos.
Falconem vocitant, equitum quo milia vicit
Dena novemque dehinc, Montem, peditumque profana.
Hoc illi vicibus peperit natale tropheum
Lux praecursoris Domini catecasta Iohannis.
Quippe latus utrimque viris comptus clipeatis
Mille legebat iter, quando tyronis ab ore
Venantis canibus lepores nemorosa per arva
Panditur adventare aequites per millia sevos.
Id scutumque simul recipit colloque pependit;   500
Armaque cum sociis stringit, penetrans inopina
Praelia. Solamen celeste petit, rapit atque
Viscera: deponunt alii clipeos animasque.
Terga parant reliqui regalibus in quibus armis
Ex pueris libuit ternis requiescere Odonis.
Tum dixit propriis: "Istos fortasse secuntur

He gathered so great a number that their count was untold:[199]
Among them were the hasty and proud Franks, their heads held high;   470
Aquitaine, you too were represented, with your sharp, barbed tongue;
The Burgundians were there; the counsel they gave was flight.
This assembly did not endure, so there was no triumph.[200]
I do not know how, but one among them, to mock his cohorts,
Slew not a small number of Danes, as fame tells us, though he had
But a few men. Like the wind he came. Ademar was his name.[201]
Then, Sclademar slit the throats of two Danes, though he perished too.[202]
He was the first to kill a Dane, sent him to Hell, when those grim
Heathens stormed the walls of Lutetia for the very first time.
He was the first to draw the sword, and in the end died by it—[203]   480
That is, his sword cut down pagans, and then a sword ran him through.
Sclademar fought beside Count Rotbert and was his retainer;[204]
His name spread dread among the Danes beneath the walls, and they fled.
Their helms, bucklers were tossed about for some three hundred leagues.
As well, a thousand less four hundred of these faithless heathens
Were struck down into the dust, in grim and fierce strife, by that
Most noble pastor Anscheric, who had with him only three
Hundred foot soldiers, as well as the power of the Virgin.[205]
Swiftly, the inhabitants ran out from the city walls, and
Brought back rich spoils that God, who reigns on high, had given to them.   490

And now, let us tell of those triumphs most worthy of Odo.
At the place called Montfaucon, he routed ten thousand horsemen
Of the heathens, and then nine thousand of their foot soldiers.[206]
He achieved this triumph on the birth anniversary of
John, who was the light that came as the herald to our Lord.
Now, as Odo was marching onwards, leading a thousand men
In arms, a young hunter met him and told him that he had seen
Hardy horsemen, approaching fast, in their thousands, just as
He chased his dogs that sought rabbits in the copses and meadows.
At these tidings, Odo seized his shield; slung it around his neck;   500
Then he gathered his arms and his men and went into combat
That he had not foreseen. He sought out Heaven's aid, then ripped out
The innards of his foes, forcing them to forsake shields and lives.
Those that remained hastily turned their backs and fled—before
A mere three young lads that bore the royal arms of Odo.
He said to his men: "It is very likely that there will be

Ast alii; idcirco pariter statum glomerate;
Si fuerit verbum super hoc, ne differat ullus."
Adiecit: "Subeam tumulum specularier ipse;
Si vos perculerit plangor, nullum mora vincat."   510
Cornu suum poscens, scopulum scandens, videt ecce
Armisonos lento pedites incedere gressu.
Tunc tuba cuius ab ore boans mox omnia late
Excitat, anfractusque per astra per arva volabant,
Omnibus atque modis, solido fractoque, ciebat.
Omne nemus responsa dabat voci famulando;
It tuba cum celeri bombo per cuncta elementa.
Nil mirum, quoniam regale caput tonat, inquam.
Ergo, sui infrenant currus, saltu quoque scandunt,
Allofilum in medium migrant, unusque securis   520
Vibratu pepulit conum de vertice regis
In humeros lapsum. Domini verum quia christum
Tundere praesumpsit, ventum de pectore iecit
Hospite continuo iaculator principis ense.
Pugna adolet, ponunt animas cum sanguine gurdi.
Infames traxere fugam, primasque tropheum.
Milia tot Foebo stravit spectante sub uno
Perpete cum gladio, donec a finibus illos
Francorum sequitur prohibet. Verum nihil illud
Ad suimet requiem iuvit, quia mox Aquitanos   530
Linquere se numenque sui postponere novit.

Appetit ergo furens illos, vastans populansque
Arva, modo vulgus; quamvis concludere nisus
Urbes adversas, minimum tamen aucta facultas.
Forte sed insurrexit eis, spreta aetheris arce
Sole sub undivaga posito testudine ponti,
Consul Ademarus regi copulatus eidem
Progenie, cuius memini. Proserpina dudum
Huic cessit, cuneos dum profligavit Odonis.
Umbra fugat stellas, Ademarus ab agmine vitas;   540
Dormit Odo, consanguineus sua proterit arma.
Astra micant, primas vigilat, sed et avolat ipsa
Regia mox consanguinitas de sanguine laeta.

Even more heathens behind us. Therefore fall into rank;
At the slightest of signals, let everyone hurry forward."
He added: "I will climb this hill myself and survey the land;
And if you hear the least noise, let no man tarry and wait."   510
He asked for his horn and climbed atop a rock—he saw a band[207]
Of foot soldiers, girt in their arms, and advancing slowly.
Then he put his horn to his mouth; its moaning call resounded
Dreadfully, near and far; rang through the fields, rose to the stars.
Its sound sometimes grew weak, faltered; sometimes rang full and clear;
And all of the forests responded with a faithful echo,
So that the call of the horn spread swiftly throughout creation.
This is not a wonder, I say, for a king sounded the call.
Then, his men seized the reins and mounted their steeds with a leap,
And galloped right into the midst of the foe. Now, a Dane swung   520
With his ax; lopped off the very tip of the royal helmet[208]
Which landed on Odo's shoulders. The Dane had presumed to strike
At the Lord's anointed. Thus was he right quickly laid low by
The sword of the king, which hacked out the soul from that heathen's breast.
The fight grew grim. Pagan lives flowed away in currents of blood.
The wretches then fled; our Prince took the prize of victory.
On that single shining of Phoebus, with his glorious sword,[209]
Odo stretched out thousands in the dust; and countless others
He chased to the far limits of Francia, and kept them out.
But he never got any rest for this work, for he soon learned   530
That Aquitaine abandoned him; denied his authority.[210]

In the year 892.
Greatly incensed, Odo marched against Aquitaine, laid it waste,
But brought not harm to many of its people, though he besieged
Cities that opposed him—however, he saw little success.[211]
One day, just as the sun had left its abode in the sky and
Went to seek refuge beneath the watery arch of the sea,
Count Ademar, whom I have already mentioned, did rise up
Against the king, even against his own blood-kin. It seemed that
Hard Proserpina heeded him, for he destroyed Odo's men.[212]
As shadows rout the stars' brightness, so Ademar routed lives.   540
While Odo slept, his faithless kinsman destroyed his warriors.
When the stars weakened, the king awoke, and his blood relative
Withdrew hastily, rejoicing in the blood that had been spilled.

Talia cur siquidem recinam congesserit olim.
Nam libuit regi dare propugnacula fratri
Rotberto Pictavis, Ademaro tamen haud sic.
Nempe sibi cepit, plus se quia diligit illo.
Inde Limovicas adiens Arvernicaque arva,
Praevalidas Wilelmi acies secum videt hostis,
Ni congressuras fluvius medio prohiberet.   550
Perdidit ergo suos illic Wilelmus honores,
Ugoni regnante datos, qui Bituricensis
Princeps extiterat consul; quare fuit actum
Hos inter geminos comites immane duellum.
Mille super centum defleverat inclitus archos
Claromontinsis Wilelmus Ugone necatos;
Iste minus numero secum maiore remotum.
Hic Ugo dum tandem capitur mucrone Wilelmi,
Supplicat, ut pietas eius succurreret illi.
Olli, tam sero per verba measse, respondit,   560
Ocius et dicto trans pectora lancea transit.
Ugonis intererant cuneis Rotgarius atque
Valde viri Stefanus fortes, perplura Wilelmi
Loeta suis dantes, alter comes Ugoniusque
Ipse nepos, alter miles Stefanus nimis audax.
Pro dolor. Ugo necem flesti, Wilelme tropheum.

Nuncius interea regalem concutit aurem;
Gallia quod mentita sibi sit portat in ore,
Gnati pressa iugo Karoli collum Lodovici,
Qui vocitatus iit celo praenomine Balbus.   570
Inde movens callem, Germanica quis sibi regna
Naviter acciperet temere disquirere vadit.
Clarus Odo castella petit vincitque duelles,
Hincce fugat Karolum facie cunctosque sequaces,
Delius ut pellit tenebras, ut Lucina athomos.
Admittit humiles dudum cervice superbos.

Sermo quis effari poterit, quotiens fuga celsi
Arnulfi induperatoris genitum tulit ense

I shall sing now of why Ademar performed these deadly deeds.
It had pleased the king to confer on Rotbert, his own brother,[213]
Whom he greatly loved, the defense of Poitiers. This did not please
Ademar at all, and so he seized the city for himself.
Thereat, Odo went to Limoges and the land of Auvergne.
Opposing him was William, who had with him his mighty host;[214]
The two would have battled had not a river stood between them.[215]   550
And so, William did not attain any honors in that place;
Instead, the king heaped honors on Hugo, who was a prince and[216]
The count also of Berry. Then, followed, between these two counts,
A bitter conflict. That famed count of Clermont, William, bewailed[217]
The loss of a thousand warriors. Hugo, too, lost many
Men—equal to the number lost by William, less a hundred.[218]
And not long afterwards, Hugo also found cause to lament,
For he was vanquished by William's sword and then captured by him.
Greatly did he beg and implore for clemency from William;
And the other replied that his words came a little too late.   560
Swifter than his words was his spear which pierced Hugo's breast.
Among the warriors of Hugo were Rotgar and Stephen;
Both were the boldest of campaigners, who had sent down to death
Many of William's men. One was a count and also Hugo's
Nephew; the other, Stephen, was a fighter most audacious.
Alas, mournful was the death of Hugo, while William triumphed.

In the years 893 and 894.
While all this was taking place, tidings came to the king's ear,
Which made known to him that Gaul had now betrayed its oath to him;[219]
Its neck was now in the yoke of Charles, the son of Louis, who
Had died and gone to heaven and was known as the Stammerer.[220]   570
Forthwith, Odo was on the march, for he hastened to find Charles,
Who had the insolence to seize the lands of Germania.[221]
He attacked the fortresses and triumphed over the rebels.[222]
He then put Charles to flight, along with those that had followed him,
Just as Delos routs the darkness and the moon melts away motes.
He did not turn away those men, once most proud but now humbled.[223]

In the year 895.
Now, who can say how often Swentibold, the son of the high[224]
Emperor Arnulf, fled before the hostile sword of Odo,

Odonis Cendebaldum post terga tonante?
Subsidium Karoli, virtus, spes hic in Odonem.   580
Cuius ad obtutus audacia non tamen umquam
Applicuit; verum nihil id requiei fuit illi.

En iterum misero gemitu loquor affore sevos
Allofilos. Terram vastant, populosque trucidant,
Circumeunt urbes pedibus, regnantis et aedes,
Ruricolas prendunt, nexant et trans mare mittunt.
Rex audit, nec curat, Odo; per verba respondit.
O, quam responsi facinus. Non ore dedisti
Tale tuo. Demon certe proprium tibi favit.
Non tua mens procurat oves Christo tibi missas.   590
Longius ille tuum forsan nec curet honorem.
Haec ubi fata receperunt probitate neglecti,
Exultant hilares, barcas agitantque per omnes
Gallia quis amnes fruitur, terram pelagusque
In dicione tenent totum, tutore ferente.

Francia, cur latitas vires, narra, peto, priscas,
Te maiora triumphasti quibus atque iugasti
Regna tibi? Propter vitium triplexque piaclum.
Quippe supercilium, Veneris quoque feda venustas
Ac vestis preciosae elatio te tibi tollunt.   600
Afrodite adeo, saltem quo arcere parentes
Haud valeas lecto, monachas Domino neque sacras.
Vel quid naturam, siquidem tibi sat mulieres,
Despicis, occurrant? Agitamus fasque nefasque.
Aurea sublimem mordet tibi fibula vestem.
Efficis et calidam tyria carnem preciosa.
Non praeter clamidem auratam cupis indusiari
Tegmine, decusata tuos gemmis nisi zona
Nulla fovet lumbos, aurique pedes nisi virgae.
Non habitus humilis, non te valet abdere vestis.   610
Haec facis. Haec aliae faciunt gentes ita nullae.
Haec tria ni linquas, vires regnumque paternum.
Omne scelus super his Christi, cuius quoque vates,
Nasci testantur bibli. Fuge, Francia, ab istis.

Which forever chased after him, roaring as if like thunder?
But in his fight against Odo, Charles saw in Swentibold hope,   580
Strength, and aid—Charles was not so brave as to face Odo alone.
But this insight brought very little comfort to Charles the king.

In the year 896.
How I groan to tell once more of the coming of the godless
Heathens. They devastated the land and slaughtered the people.[225]
They swarmed into towns and into the royal residences.
They seized peasants, put them in chains, and sent them over the sea.
King Odo heard of this, but he cared not—he said as much.
O, what a base, shameful response! Surely, this could not have come
From your mouth. Certainly, it was the Devil that spoke through you;
How could your spirit neglect the sheep Christ put in your care?   590
Perhaps you shall not preserve your own honor for much longer.
In time, when this remark was reported to the heathen foe,
They rejoiced and exulted and let their ships wander through
All the rivers that water Gaul, and held sway on land and sea.
And he, who was our protector, allowed this to happen.[226]

O France, tell me, I pray you, what became of your strength and might,
With which you once could overcome and subdue kingdoms that were
Often far stronger than you? Your weakness has come from three sins:[227]
The first is pride, which leads you to the rank pleasures of Venus
And to wear costly clothes. These things have exhausted your strength.   600
Aphrodite holds such sway over you that you cannot keep
Mothers from your bed, nor nuns consecrated to our Lord.[228]
And why do you indulge in acts contrary to nature when
Women yearn for your touch? We just do things whether good or not.
An extravagant golden fibula holds your cloak in place;
Clothes meant just to keep you warm you dye in Tyrian purple.[229]
No mantle covers you if it is not richly worked with gold;
No belt shall girt your loins if it is not encrusted with gems;
And the lachets of your shoes must also always be golden.
Being without humility, you cannot wear humble clothes.   610
This is how you are—and no other nation acts as you do.
These three sins you must forsake, or lose the land of your fathers.
They indeed are the source of all vice, as the books of old and
The Prophets that heralded Christ attest. Flee, O France, from them.

Psallere non tedet. Defit tamen actus Odonis
Nobilis, is quanquam mulcet superas adhuc auras.
Flagito, quo positor possim per amena polorum
Hoste canas, lector, gratarier atria victo.

EXPLICIT SECUNDUS
PARISIACAE URBIS BELLORUM PRESULISQUE GERMANI
MIRACULORUM LIBELLUS.

I have not grown weary of singing—only now the deeds of
The noble Odo fail me—though the land still finds joy in him.[230]
I beg you, O reader, pray for me, the poet, that I be
Granted strength to rout the Foe, and live in Heaven's great mansions.[231]

HERE ENDS THE SECOND BOOK OF THE BATTLES
OF THE CITY OF PARIS,
ALONG WITH THE MIRACLES OF BISHOP GERMAIN.

INGREDITUR TERTIUS CLERICORUM SCILICET DECUS TYRUNCULORUMQUE EFFECTUS.

Clerice, dipticas lateri ne dempseris umquam;
Corcula labentis fugias ludi fore, ne te
Laetetur foedus sandapila neque toparcha.
Machia sit tibi, quo ierarchia, necque cloaca.
Non enteca nec alogia, verum absida tecum
Conmaneat, mentes, acrimonia, non quia mordet.
Agoniteta tuus fiat ambusilla tui mens
Ne uranium praeter cromam legat, is quia multis
Esse deus solet. Anodiam sectare gemellam.
Sistere sincophanta verere, boba tamen adsis.   10
Gripphia te tangat, carchesia togaque crebro.
Grammaton sinteca frequens sistat tibi; longe,
Absistat vero glaucoma, criminis offa.
Brathea blatta dehinc, enclitica prosapiaque
Militiae Christi per te nullatenus absint.
Amphytappa laon extat badanola necnon;
Effipiam diamant, stragulam pariterque propomam.
Agagulam caelebs aginat, pecudes nec ablundam.
Effipia et stragula praetexta est aulica cura.
Utitur anabola mulier, sed abutitur ipsa.   20
Convenit invalidis apozima nec ne placenta.
Cleronome, Codrus maneas unaque disertus.
Cum fisco teneas yppos; uxorius haud sis.
Nomine limphatici careas, crisostomus ut sis;
Apocrisarus ades, aforismos os tibi servet.
Basileus constes, abstemius antigraphusque;
Cosmographus, solumque tui catasscopus esto.
Gimnus ab inlicitis, ne sisque biotticus actor.
Acrizimum celebres; oroscopus esque didasclus.
Inque thoro amphyballum habeas, effebus et absit.   30
Canterus adsit habunde tibi, sed amasius absit.
Cerritus caveas fore, perifrasticus atque.
Abbachus manui, niteatque teologus ori.
Baccaulum fauste videas te ferre cloacae.
Prodigus, obliqus, monotalmus, subdolus haud sis.

HERE BEGINS THE THIRD BOOK, THAT IS, FOR THE USE OF CLERICS, AND FOR THE BENEFIT OF NOVICES.

O cleric, do not forget the counsel found in these verses,
Lest you become the accompanist to untamed revelers
And become the Devil's delight, the base joy of the bier.[232]
Fight in the realm of holiness, not before the walls of Hell.[233]
Savor not the treasure chest or high feasts, but forever keep
Lucid perception with you, which cannot seize and taint the heart.[234]
Make the stomach your soldier so that your heart will not take on
A color that is any other than that of Heaven, which
For most becomes a false god. Search and find out that double cure.[235]
Do not become a flatterer; thus you shall always be strong.   10
Hold firm to the Scriptures, to the chalice and priestly vestments.[236]
Engage frequently in the exercise of writing, and thus
Chase away foul swellings and specks that come to impede the eye.[237]
Put aside the plates of gold and the purple robes—choose meekness.
Thus, shall you never stray far from the bold warriors of Christ.[238]
Let the laymen have their woolen hangings, their fine beds,
For they value costly bedclothes, bright apparel, and strong drinks.
The wise man abides not among pimps, with their herds and dross.[239]
Fine-cut robes and vivid coverings belong in the palace.
A stole can adorn a woman, but she makes ill use of it.[240]   20
Herbals and brews and porridges are suitable for the sick.[241]
O inheritor, be like Codrus, and a forceful poet.[242]
To guide a horse, you grab its balls; handle a woman likewise.[243]
Do not babble like the insane, but acquire a golden mouth.[244]
Become a thoughtful minister and speak words that are sermons.
Stand like a king most sober, and behave like an advocate.
Be skilled as a geographer, an explorer of yourself.[245]
Shun immoral nakedness; nor be a player in the world.
Eat more of slightly leavened bread; heed time, and be a teacher.
Your bed covers should be rough; bring not beardless boys there.   30
Surround yourself with geldings that you might not take on lovers.[246]
Take heed not to become frenzied and ramble on forever;
Rather be that tablet on which is written the word of God.[247]
Thus shall you be borne on the bier in honor to your grave.
Be not a glutton, nor pretend, nor be purblind, nor faithless.

Ludibrium vites, baratrum; sectare tropheum.
Amphyteatra procul tibi stent, egilopia necnon.
Nam scrupulum generant ΨΙΧΗ vexantque pupillas.
Scandito analogium, crisis nitet ore docentis.
Declina birotum, bravium capito ac cliotedrum.   40
Culleum habe, diametra scias, ergastula nesci.
Exares emistichium, cum distica sculpes.
Enoforo liba; lotium laxare suesce.
Dilige tu xenodochium, zelotipiaque odi.
Hinc acitabula doma tuum seu congia stringat.
Pomerium curti, pomaria congrua malis.
Fulgeat ecclesiis ostrum, longe sit oletum.
Praedia quala tibi statuant, agitent flabra flagra.
Eminus ut gorgon fugiat, pota diamoron.
Sperne platon olon, sinposia, quatinus odon   50
Te lustret. Temeson vigeas, si non potes insons.
Lar tibi, quo nectar fraglet, lucarque nec absit.
Gallonis memor esto tui; ambro timeto cieri.
Mulio strabo tuus neque sit neque agason inermis.
Abbaso quo fuerit, sit hirudo frequens comitata.
Disparet ac validos intercapedo citatim,
Si qua virago tuum penetret, reminiscere, doma.
Bule tegat Christi mentem tibi, gausape mensam.
Entole te comat, regesque baben proceresque.
Abdomen minime superet corpus, mage teche.   60
Uranei neotericus atque neofitus haud sis
Dogmatis ac fidei, iugiter sed priscus ab olim.
Quattuor immo tuum hec ut iter comitentur in aevum:
Teche Dei, ieron, archonque, palinodianque.
Ancisus vivas, quin cardiacus moriare.
Ceruleas vestes si gestas, posce colimbum.
Ducitur anquina limbus, arcippio necnon.
Canterus antelis et postelis equitatur.
Aporiam, sed et atrophiam, patiaris, ut acam
Atervam appodix tua mens sibi congerat eius.   70
Algemam mentis anquirunt talia; verum
Aphatiam amendant, anteceniam quoque largam
Edificant. Agapem suffert agape nimis apta.

Avoid lewd cavorting—and Hell; seek the honors of victors.[248]
Do not go to see spectacles which shall surely bring you harm;
They will blight not only your eyes but also blemish your soul.
Ascend to the dais; the teacher's mouth is ever golden.[249]
Shun the chariot of lust and pride; receive the crown and throne.[250]   40
Hide away filth; heed passing time, and thus banish dishonor.
Always be mindful of half-verses when you craft poetry.[251]
If you tip the wine jug often, you will have to piss often.
Be fond of the humble dwelling place, and come to hate hatred.[252]
Do not let your house become filled with wine and lilting music.
Free land befits the court, as apples belong to the orchard.[253]
Purple should shimmer in churches; shit should be flung far away.[254]
In fields you shall find baskets—the wind sets all the reeds astir.
To ward against snakes, drink black mulberry juice, mixed with honey.
Spurn filth and boisterous revels—thus shall you find the true path.   50
Better to be half-guilty if you cannot be innocent.
May you have a full, fragrant larder, the forest-levy's wealth.[255]
Take care when dealing with hired hands; fear wastefulness.
A drover should not be squint-eyed, nor should a hostler lack arms.
The physician should be found not far from the infirmary.
Spurn long phases of inactivity; be strong and mobile.
Take care that a shrewish woman does not enter your house.
Let the words of Christ drape your mind, as a cloth drapes your table.
Don holy commandments; let kings don their jeweled necklets.[256]
Let holy words and instruction increase your girth, and not fat.   60
Be not a stranger to holiness, nor a beginner in
Matters of your faith, but be wise as the ancients from the past.
Always maintain these four close at hand, never stray far from them:
Resounding praise, an upright priest, the king, and the word of God.[257]
Live a life of discipline that you may not die of heart-strain.[258]
If your clothing is dirty and stained, then seek out a washtub.
A rope will pull away a boat, but a string will pull the bow.[259]
Ride a horse with a saddle securely girt both front and back.
Endure both hardship and poverty so that your soul, which is
Your companion, may gather for itself eternal joy.   70
Strive to make the heart suffer; it will defeat all indolence,
And then you shall win for yourself the greatest of all rewards.[260]
Perfect love can endure the suffering brought on by others.

Nisibus aegidiam in giro secteris acutis.
Agnatos teneas, aregidiam quoque verbi
Anheles, hostis ne sis atratus in aslum.
Aulea ne angustent animam sceleris, sed aprilax
Alluat aethereus, noxis ne apostata fias.
Leva ancile geras, dextra agoniamque fidei.
Auspicio amaneas. Apogeum aliquam ampliet altum.   80
Armenum cordi tollas, arcisterium addas.
Architriclinus amicale amineum colit, atque
Huic malis etiam apofereta autumnus honustat.
Antropus ast agamus caelibatum colat, et sic
Argiripam cernet patriam civesque beatos.
Haud huic est apoplexia cure, sed et astu
Angustat nullos, amarthetes solet idem
Antiquare, aginat venerem, anaboladia portat.
Alburnis albent pomis huic apofereta.
Virtutes cunctae comitantur amiciter illum.   90
Hunc non allidunt affurcillando sinistri.
E Baccho quoniam bittunt geniti bibiones,
Blatterat amineo si constiterint et eidem
Indignum referens brancho prorsusque brutescit;
Haud illa bittit, quo quisquis honore bimetur.
Burra, probum fateor buteonem, qui arva bidentat;
Hic sed et ingenuus similem retinent genituram.
Buggeus apparat et burgos, verum biliosus.
Apparat atque bosor taphium sibi, sed biliosum;
Sic animae corpus vita conponit atratum,   100
Laeta sed Omnipotens, si mens felix, parat astra;
Comiter hoc cunctos moneas tu, miles herilis.
Praeterea, cum quis noxam clandestinat, antro
Cespitat, atque coagmentat si crimina; virtus
Communit mentem, coalescit comiter eius
Pectoris in portu clandestina; nam cluit illic
Clancule; non constare diu tamen ipsa valebit
Clancula, teste tonante super sacrata per ora.
Cum videas astum pessumdare saecla nefandum,
Immo clientelae tutor Domini velut haeres   110
Hic maneas, clivos virtutum quatinus almos

You can only chase after the she-goat of lust round and round.[261]
Hold fast to close kinsmen, and forever desire for the rain
Of God's Word, that you may not become plunder for the Devil.[262]
Do not let the veil of wickedness enshroud your soul; rather,
Let Heaven's love pour on your soul that you might be free of sin.
Bear the shield of rousing faith; with your right hand fight with joy.
Do not venture close to augury—deep caves hide evil seeds.   80
Lift off the veil from your heart—go hide in the monastery.
The lord of the house happily brings in white wine, and even
Autumn weighs him down with great bushels of apples piled so high.
A man who is without a wife should practice good chastity;
Thus shall he come dwell in his native city with the blessed.[263]
He is not afraid of dying suddenly—indeed there
Is nothing he has not pruned wisely; the wretched he has brought
Back to their former vigor—lust he has driven away,
And he dons friendship's garb—a bounty of sweet apples is his.[264]
All virtues are at his side as his happy companions;   90
Now, evil desires cannot assault and subjugate him.
But if he allows Bacchus to infiltrate his white wine with
The foul worm, then shall his tongue become tainted with great folly,[265]
And sinking to the level of the brute he shall let his mouth
Blaspheme. But he who has nurtured honor cannot suffer thus.
The righteous youth is he who goes out and tends the darkest field;[266]
And in this way he becomes an equal of the high-born man.
The eunuch is happy with his bright castle, but the man full
Of sorrow knows the truth and instead works to build his sad grave.[267]
Though the flesh is formed to bring anguish to the soul, yet has the   100
Almighty readied bliss amidst the stars, for the pure of heart.
O soldier of the Lord, go spread this joyful message to all.
Now, if any man seeks to hide a sin, it is as if he
Had fallen into a deep chasm, and sin grows triumphant.
But virtue can strengthen the mind and secretly, most gently
Come to fill the heart; great is its might when it remains hidden;[268]
And yet this concealed virtue cannot remain strong for too long,
As the thundering mouths of the blessed saints often affirm.
Whenever you see wickedness and cunning consume the world,
Become the protector of the faithful, and remain among   110
Men as the servant of the Lord; thus shall you reach the most high

Scandere concinnas ΘΗΟ tu clangere laudes
Nomine sistenti ternis valeas, modo soli
Magestate tamen nutu doxaque perhenni.
Quam pariter tecum teneam, tu clerice poscas.

FINITUR CERNUI OPUSCULUM CATECASTI EXIMII
CONFESSORIS GERMANI
SUGGESTUSQUE PARISIACI PRAELII HUMILLIMIQUE
LEVITAE ABBONIS.

Places of virtue, forever chanting the praises of God,[269]
Who abides always three in number, yet forever but one,
Whose majesty, Whose might, Whose glory is indeed without end.
Pray, O good cleric, that I may come to this glory with you.

HERE ENDS THIS LITTLE BOOK OF THE WORTHY
AND HOLY CONFESSOR GERMAIN,
ALONG WITH THE COMPILATION OF THE BATTLES OF PARIS,
BY THE HUMBLE AND LOWLY ABBO.

NOTES TO THE TRANSLATION

[1] This Gozlin, perhaps a fellow monk at the abbey, is not to be confused with Bishop Gozlin, who died in 886, during the siege of Paris, as mentioned later in Book Two, lines 70–71. Bishop Gozlin was also the Abbot of Saint-Germain-des-Prés.

[2] Here, we have the move to a specific and salvific notion of history, wherein God's redemptive purpose is to be witnessed.

[3] Abbo tells us that this poem is largely unedited, and therefore filled with shortcomings. Aside from typical writerly humility, this is also an attempt to explain why his revered teacher Aimoin did not like this work, as Abbo tells us later in the letter.

[4] One of the attributes of the god Apollo was reason. The use of Grecian terms was fashionable in Carolingian times, as is plentifully evident in Abbo's work. Although Greek vocabulary was fairly extensive in this era, the proper understanding of the language was lacking in Western Europe. Abbo probably acquired his Greek terminology from the Latin-Greek glossary of Philoxenus, a copy of which certainly existed in the Abbey of Saint-Germain-des-Prés; it was lost sometime after 1573 when Henri Estienne published his *Glossaria*. See *Glossae latinograecae et graecolatinae*, Corpus Glossariorum Latinorum 2, ed. Georg Goetz and Gotthold Gundermann (Leipzig: B.G. Teubner, 1888), esp. vii–xix.

[5] Virgil was well known and influential in Abbo's time, as his comment attests. See John J. Contreni, *Codex Laudunensis 468: A Ninth-Century Guide to Virgil, Sedulius, and the Liberal Arts* (Turnhout: Brepols, 1984); Raymond Cornier, "A Preliminary Checklist of Early Medieval Glossed Vergil Manuscripts," *Studi Medievali* 32 (1991): 971–9, and, of course, *The Sankt Gall Priscian Commentary*, ed. Rijcklof Hofman (Münster: Nodus, 1996).

[6] This comment serves to highlight the serious and widespread nature of the Viking threat in West Francia.

[7] Silenus, the teacher of the god Dionysus, was said to be not only the wisest but also the most drunken of the followers of the god, and therefore a master of revels.

[8] Orpheus, the legendary poet and musician, was also the inventor of the lyre. He went to the underworld to bring back his love, Eurydice, by the power of his song. He lost her when he transgressed the stipulated rules of the "rescue" set down by Hades, or Orcus, the god of the underworld—that is, he looked back to see if Eurydice did indeed follow him. Tartarus is the underworld.

[9] Abbo marks a crucial difference between the task of the poet, which is to invent, and that of the historian, which is to relate and interpret. This argument of the inability of poets to grasp truth, of course, is borrowed from Plato via Socrates in *The Apology* (22a–b). A good translation is found in *The Last Days of Socrates: Euthyphro, Apology, Crito, Phaedo*, trans. Hugh Tredennick and Harold Tarrant (London: Penguin, 2003).

[10] Germain (496–576) became bishop of Paris in 555 and remained in that office until his death.

[11] The complete manuscript in the *Bibliothèque nationale de France* (MS lat. 13833) is perhaps in Abbo's own hand.

[12] The various caesuras Abbo mentions are peculiar to Latin hexameter verse. The penthemimeral caesura (rest or pause) is a common one and occurs after the fifth half-foot. The hepthemimeral caesura is found after the first half of the fourth foot. The Bucolic caesura (also known as dieresis) acquired its name because of its frequent use in Classical Bucolic verse; it is found at the end of a complete word of the fourth foot. A dieresis marks that place in a hexameter where a foot and a word end together. Episynaloephe is a sort of metaplasm, wherein two syllables are brought together, rather than omitting one or the other. A catalectic line is metrically incomplete.

[13] The teacher is Aimoin, a monk at Saint-Germain-des-Prés, mentioned earlier.

[14] Lutetia is the Roman name for Paris. There is currently much debate as to whether the Roman city was in fact located on the Île-de-la-Cité, where sparse Roman remains are to be found; there are only the arena near Montparnasse and the baths, which are now part of the Musée de Cluny. However, some ten kilometers to the West, in Nanterre, extensive ruins of a city have recently been discovered, suggesting that Roman Lutetia might well have been located there. See Jean-Pierre Dubois, "La découverte d'une cité gauloise à Nanterre remet en cause la localisation de Lutèce sur L'Île-de-la-Cité," *Le Monde* (February 27, 2004): 24. The traditional view is expounded in Philippe de Carbonnières, *Lutèce: Paris ville romaine* (Paris: Gallimard, 2001), and in Jean-Pierre Adam, *Les thermes antiques Lutèce* (Paris: Réunion des musées nationaux, 1996).

[15] Isia is likely Hysia, a town on the Theban plain, below Mount Cithairon, mentioned for example by Euripides (*The Bacchae*, line 751). Abbo's notion that Isia is an older name for Paris is nothing but convenient poetic etymology.

[16] Abbo is foreshadowing the greedy lust of the Danes for the riches of Paris, by drawing out a classical allusion to the desire of the Argives to conquer Hysia; the harbor of that ancient Greek city mirrors the fine bridges of Paris.

[17] Abbo is assuming, as medieval etymologies often did, that *Paris* is a corrupted form of *Isia* (Hysia).

[18] *Sequanus* is the Gallo-Roman designation for the Seine, and perhaps derives from the name of the goddess Sequana, to whom the river was sacred; or the name could simply mean "sacred stream" in Gallic. Hydronyms are notoriously difficult to pin down accurately when it comes to meaning. See Robert V. Houssa, *Étude de l'hydronymie européene* (Brussels: R.V. Houssa, 1982).

[19] The "island" is the Île-de-la-Cité.

[20] Pluto is the Roman equivalent of Hades. By Christian times, he came to be associated with Satan because of his abode in the underworld. Abbo sees the Vikings as the minions of the Devil—that is, they are the embodiment of demonic forces bent on destroying Christian civilization (Paris). Bishop Gozlin might have been the bastard son of Louis the Pious; more likely he was the son Roricon, count of Maine. He was once a captive of the Vikings and was released only after the payment of a heavy ransom. He also served as a chancellor for Charles the Bald. He was elected bishop of Paris in 883 or 884, and was active in the defense of the city when the Norsemen attacked. He died in 886, perhaps from plague that broke out during the ensuing siege.

[21] Abbo constructs an interesting narrative trope whereby the true audience of his epic poem is the personified city of Paris.

[22] A fleet of seven hundred ships sailing on the Seine is an exaggeration. See Carroll Gillmor, "War on the Rivers: Viking Numbers and Mobility on the Seine and Loire, 841–886," *Viator* 19 (1988): 79–109, esp. 86. Whatever the accurate number, Abbo's concern is other than precision, a concept very foreign to the medieval historian. The point is that the Vikings have appeared in a number far greater than the two hundred defenders inside Paris; and more importantly, the assaults on the faithful are dire. Exaggeration allows for the highlighting of the power and heroism of Saint Germain and the valor of Count Odo and the many Frankish warriors.

[23] Abbo picks up on the impermanent quality of Viking leaders. Indeed, Siegfried is not a king, but more a chieftain, chosen by election to lead a band of raiders in looting expeditions. There is also that rather famous reply by Rollo's Vikings on the Seine when a Frankish messenger asks to speak to their leader. "What is the name of your leader?" he asks. The Vikings reply, "No one, we all hold equal power here." This remark is found in Dudo of St. Quentin, *De moribus et actis primorum Normanniae Ducum auctore Dudone Sancti Quintini Decano*, ed. Jules Lair (Caen: Société des antiquaries de Normandie, 1865), 154.

[24] Odo's nobility is such that it is recognized even by someone Abbo would deem savage and uncivilized. There is also a tinge of prophecy in that a pagan perceives the future (royal) worth of Odo.

[25] It is obvious that either Siegfried or Bishop Gozlin can speak the other's tongue. The question of communication between the roving bands of Vikings and the Franks is an interesting one and deserves greater exploration—especially the notion of translation at this time. Certainly the Frankish and Norse languages were akin.

[26] Rotbert (the Frankish form of "Robert") was Odo's younger brother. Ragenar, or Regnier, known as "Long Neck," was the count of Hainault. Ebolus became the abbot of Saint-Germain-des-Prés in 881, after his uncle Gozlin became bishop. Perhaps the wound that Abbo mentions here was another the cause of Bishop Gozlin's death later on during the siege, if he did not die of the plague.

[27] The identity of Frederick cannot be determined.

[28] It is important to note that Abbo consistently interweaves the divine with the mundane.

[29] "Ultimate Thule" is a cliché for an island in the far North. Pliny the Elder describes it in his *Natural History*, IV, Book XVI, 104.

[30] "Crenels" for the original *fenestris*. This refers to the stone tower in front of the Grand Pont.

[31] The Viking ballistae were tension trebuchets, or throwing engines, which could hurl either stones or javelins.

[32] The humor of this comment likely lies in the fact that Vikings were very careful about their personal appearance, and took great pride in washing and grooming their hair and beards daily; they were also said to bathe every Saturday. Perhaps Abbo and the other Parisians witnessed their regular preening. See Gwyn Jones, *A History of the Vikings* (Oxford: Oxford University Press, 1968), 177. There is also Ibn Fadlan's famous and notorious passage on the curious washing habits of the Norsemen he encountered; this account is found in H.M. Smyser's "Ibn Fadlan's Account of the Rus, With Some Commentary and Some Allusions to *Beowulf*," in *Franciplegius: Medieval and Linguistic Studies in Honor of Francis Peabody Magoun, Jr.*, ed. Jess B. Bessinger, Jr., and Robert P. Creed (New York: New York University Press, 1965), 92–119.

[33] Ebolus has skewered the Vikings, just as pieces of flesh or some chickens are skewered before being roasted. We have a visual record of what Ebolus might have meant in the Bayeux Tapestry, in the cooking and serving of a feast at Hastings. Here, we note as well the concern for cleanliness, with the kneeling steward holding a bowl of water, with a towel draped over his left arm. See Andrew Bridgeford, *1066: The Hidden History of the Bayeux Tapestry* (London and New York: Fourth Estate, 2004), scenes 38 and 39. Also Mogens Rud, *The Bayeux Tapestry and the Battle of Hastings 1066* (Copenhagen: Christian Eilers, 1992), 70–1.

[34] These figures are exaggerated in order to show the divine agency at work (or that of Saint Germain): although the faithful number only two hundred, they can turn aside a host of infidels numbering in the thousands.

[35] Ceres is the Roman goddess of grain; Bacchus, of course, is the god of wine; and boar meat was part of a splendid feast in Germanic tradition. The wives' complaint stems from the notion that they have given their men the best to eat and have gotten only cowardice in return.

[36] This goading is interesting because it prefigures one of the roles assumed by women in Icelandic sagas, that of the inciter who urges men into action—usually an action the men are reluctant to undertake and that involves violence. For example, there is the famous incident in Section 116 of the *Njal's Saga*, where Hildigunn goads Flosi to avenge Hoskuld, her slain husband. See *Njal's Saga*, ed. Carl F. Bayerschmidt and Lee M. Hollander (Ware, Herfordshire: Wordsworth Editions, 1998), 227–9. For an overview of this role of women, see Michael Murphy, "Vows, Boasts and Taunts, and the Role of Women in Some Medieval Literature," *English Studies* 66 (1985): 105–12. Useful also is Ward Parks, "Flyting, Sounding, Debate: Three Verbal Contest Genres," *Poetics Today* 7 (1986): 439–58.

[37] For the Romans, Bellona personified the battle frenzy of Mars.

[38] Could this be the earliest reference to the Oriflamme, the sacred banner of the French? Abbo's description certainly adheres to the traditional depiction of later accounts, from the twelfth century onwards. See Anne Lombard-Jourdan, *Fleur de lis et oriflamme: signes célestes du royaume de France* (Paris: Presses du CNRS, 1991).

39 Lemnos is the Aegean island where tradition located the forge of Hephaestos (or Vulcan), god of fire. Neptune, of course, is the god of the sea.

40 Rotbert, a Frankish warrior, whose identity is otherwise not known. Presumably, these quick sketches of warriors are also a summary of their personalities, which would allow for their recognition by Abbo's contemporaries.

41 Charon is the ferryman of the dead, who bears souls across the River Acheron into the infernal regions. Abbo persistently describes the souls of the Vikings as inhabiting Hades, the pagan Hell. Thus, he emphasizes the wretched lot of the pagan Danes, who live and die outside of God's redemptive plan. Such classical allusions further underscore the otherness of the Danes.

42 This is quite an accurate description of a Viking encampment, with earthworks and dikes. See Eric Carl Oxenstierna, *The World of the Norsemen* (London: Weidenfeld & Nicolson, 1967), 138–9.

43 "Alps" is not a geographically specific term; rather the meaning is "mountains" in general. The reference to befouling associates the Vikings with defilement and blasphemy—a notion that Abbo will explore more fully later on when he describes the ransacking of the churches, especially his own abbey of Saint-Germain-des-Prés.

44 Fleeing from the path of the marauding Norsemen was the usual mode of preservation for those in monasteries, abbeys, and smaller villages. Abbo laments this lack of resistance, since it has put the onus on Paris, which must endure the savagery of the Vikings alone. There is certainly validity in reading the entire first book as the "Passion of Paris."

45 Vikings often used battering rams against fortified cities. Abbo's description is very accurate; the sixteen wheels would be used in sequences of threes, with one wheel at the front, which served as a support for the ram itself. See Bernard Bachrach, *Early Carolingian Warfare* (Philadelphia: University of Philadelphia Press, 2001), 116. Useful also is Helen J. Nicholson, *Medieval Warfare: Theory and Practice of War, 300–1500* (Houndsmills, England; New York: Palgrave Macmillan, 2004), 88–112.

46 The fact that the force of the javelin pierces two Danes suggests that it is shot by a ballista; such war engines would have been mounted on the walls of Paris. The term "javelin" is a translation of *fala* in the original, which has led some to construe another meaning, based upon the term *falarica*, that is, a projectile set alight before being hurled by a catapult. However, Abbo, who is generally very specific about fire, makes no mention of a "flaming dart." Carroll Gillmor, "The Introduction of the Traction Trebuchet into the Latin West," *Viator* 12 (1981): 1–8, sees a *falarica* here rather than a *fala*.

47 Here, Abbo describes a "cat," which was a wooden structure on wheels, with a blue-hide covering, beneath which the Vikings could approach the walls. The rawhide would not only deflect arrows, but would also be impervious to fire.

48 *Pluteos*, or *pluteus*, means "shelter," while *crates* or *cratis* refers to the hurdle or wickerwork around which fabric was draped to serve as a shelter. This suggests that some of the protective housings were of wattle-and-daub, which again would be difficult to set alight. We cannot be certain to which "Latin writer" Abbo refers. Perhaps Vegetius or even Julius Caesar.

49 Phoebus, the sun god, rides a *quadrigae*, a chariot drawn by four horses.

50 That is, *proles Satanae*. This is the first time that Abbo specifically links the Vikings with Satan, a view theologically sound for his time, since the Church maintained that pagan religions were created by the Devil to lead humankind astray. Psalm 96:5 was often used in support of this view. Also, a similar view is expounded a few centuries earlier by Pope Gregory in his letter to Abbot Mellitus on the heathen practices of the newly converted English (as preserved in Bede's *Ecclesiastical History of the English People*, Book I, chap. 30).

51 This is a curious comparison, especially since bees were largely seen in a positive light in medieval literature and were an example of consistent industry. It is likely that the fury of the Vikings is compared to the rage of a disturbed swarm of bees. From the walls of Paris, Danes perhaps also look like bees, with their bows slung over the shoulder that remind Abbo of wings—a peculiar anthropomorphism at play, nevertheless.

52 The "pots with molten lead" would be grenades, of sorts, lobbed over the walls to start fires, while stones from catapults would raze the fortified turrets on the very top of the bridges.

53 Rotbert is Odo's brother, mentioned already in line 67 above. Ragenar is the count of Hainault also mentioned in the same line. Utto is perhaps a member of Bishop Gozlin's retinue; he is mentioned again in Book I, line 653. He is not to be confused with Count Odo. The identity of Erilang is unknown.

54 The Vikings head for the Grand Pont and its tower. Perhaps "painted ships" refers to the brightly painted shields that were hung along the gunwales of Norse ships.

55 Abbo completes the image he introduced earlier of the Vikings as vicious bees; here they unleash their "stings," in effect.

56 This suggests that the Vikings are far more organized than often implied and assumed by Abbo; they are not simply a swarming horde, but a well-organized body of besiegers.

57 Abbo's concern is larger than giving an eyewitness report; he is, rather, a witness to divine intrusion into history.

58 These are the "cats" mentioned earlier, lines 217–20.

59 The original reads *fele*, or "gall," which can perhaps be identified either with wolfsbane or hemlock. The implication is that the Vikings dipped their arrowheads in some sort of poison, which would kill an individual, even if the wound were superficial.

60 The *testudo*, or "tortoise," was a typical protective formation used by the Romans, which Abbo might have read about in classical sources (Vegetius, Polybius or Livy, for example). A *testudo* consisted of a formation of soldiers in close order, who used their shields to protect the integrity of this unit—front, back, sides and overhead. Given the context, a "cat" might also be meant by the term *testudo*, the construction of which has already been described.

61 These trenches are defensive dikes dug before the walls of Paris.

62 A very clever commentary on Psalm 9:15. Again, for Abbo, actions taking place in the world can only be understood as epiphanic instances of the divine.

63 This recalls the celestial hierarchy as expounded by Pseudo-Dionysus the Areopagite, which is comprised of three levels. Thrones are part of the first hierarchy, Virtues and Dominions are part of the second, and Principalities belong to the third. There is also scriptural endorsement of this schema, with which Abbo would have been perfectly familiar, namely, Ephesians 6:12 and Colossians 1:16. See also S. Lilla, "Note sulla Gerarchia Celeste dello Ps. Dionigi l'Areopagita," *Augustinianum* 26 (1986): 519–73.

64 Such extended hymns of praise, as well as prayers, were often included in the later *chansons de geste*, especially before a fateful battle.

65 Paris sits within seven hills, a feature that links it to Rome, thus bestowing on it a special, or even holy, mission and status—very much in keeping with Abbo's larger agenda of describing the convergence of the sacred with the everyday.

66 A mangonel was a torsion catapult designed to fire heavy darts or stones.

67 This conflagration signals a shift in the poem; hereafter, magical realism purposefully enters into the narrative.

68 Saint Germain is traditionally invoked against fire. Abbo is setting up a demonstration of divine intervention.

69 "Carts," like "cats," are covered shelters for approaching the walls of a city in relative safety during a siege.

70 A *carcamusa* was a metal-tipped ram, mounted on wheels.

71 Abbo consistently anthropomorphizes the walls and towers of Paris. Through this device, the assaults come to be depicted as a collective attack on Christian civilization, on the Christian body.

72 That is, on February 2, 886.

73 That is, Francia, or the region that lay East of Paris and North of the Seine.

[74] Rotbert the Quiver was the count of Troyes ca. 876–886; he was married to Gisela, the daughter of Louis the Stammerer. Abbo describes his heroic death, which occurred in 886.

[75] This is the same Adalhelm who is mentioned later in Book II, line 209. Given Germanic fostering traditions, Adalhelm is likely the son of Rotbert's sister.

[76] That is, the abbey and church of Saint-Germain-des-Prés, which was located in a meadow on the right bank of the Seine. Saint Germain was interred there in 576, in the adjoining chapel of Saint Symphorien. The church, which was built in 588, at the orders of King Childebert, was originally dedicated to Saint Vincent, since it held this saint's stole as a relic. In 754, Germain was canonized and his body buried inside the church proper, at which time it was also dedicated to him and renamed in his honor. In attendance, at this ceremony, was the seven-year old Charlemagne.

[77] The Eumenides or Furies tormented the guilty in classical mythology. The Dane's guilt is desecration.

[78] The church being Saint-Germain-des-Prés. Abbo shows how effectively the Saint protects his property and his believers.

[79] The parents of Saint Germain were buried alongside him in Saint-Germain-des-Prés. Both Eleutherius and Eusebia were natives of Autun, where Germain was born. All three tombs were destroyed during the French Revolution.

[80] This is the Petit Pont on the left bank, which was made of wood. This event occurred on February 6, 886.

[81] The bridge would be to the right of the city of Paris, if viewed from Saint-Germain-des-Prés. Presumably, Abbo was inside the city walls and not in the abbey, which had been abandoned when the Vikings struck—still Abbo prefers to give the perspective with which he would have been familiar, rather than the one he might have had from the city walls.

[82] This tower is the one in front of the Grand Pont.

[83] The earth, being God's creation, laments along with the Franks, who are God's people. Abbo unites the natural world with the Christian faith, just as he anthropomorphizes the city of Paris and makes it weep and mourn along with her inhabitants.

[84] A plaque of marble can still be seen near the entrance to the Petit Pont, on which are inscribed the names of these twelve brave Frankish warriors, who are otherwise unknown. It is significant that Abbo numbers these valiant warriors as twelve—firstly, because this recalls the twelve Disciples, and secondly, in Germanic tradition a lord was often surrounded by a band of twelve faithful retainers (the *comitatus*).

[85] These catapults are on the parapet of the tower in front of the Grand Pont.

[86] Hawks and warriors are closely associated in Germanic literature. See for example, *The Saga of Rolf Kraki*, chap. 40, *The Saga of Olaf Haraldson*, chap. 90, and the Old English poems *The Battle of Maldon*, line 8, and *Beowulf*, line 2263.

[87] That is, Saint Germain.

[88] That is, the blaze is stronger than the water. Vulcan, the god of fire and the forge, limped—a characteristic of most gods of the smithy in Indo-European lore; for example, Weland the Smith.

[89] Pluto is the classical god of the dead and ruler of Hades. As pagans, Abbo sees this as a fitting abode for the Vikings. Perhaps there is also an echo of Valhalla, the great hall of the slain, in which Odin serves up a feast for the heroic dead, cooked up in the cauldron called Eldhrimnir.

[90] This Eriveus is the one mentioned previously in line 525. However, in the manuscript their names are spelled differently: *Erveus* here and *Eriveus* earlier. But given the context, they are one and the same.

[91] That is, the glorious deeds and deaths of the twelve shall only be forgotten when the sun shines at night and when the moon and the stars appear during the day. This metaphor for impossibility includes the suggestion that human memory is eternal—especially if we bear in mind, as noted already, that the number twelve is fraught with theological and cultural connotations.

[92] This is the tower that stood in front of the Petit Pont on the left bank.

[93] Presumably, Abbo refers to a man whom he does not name, who fought alongside the twelve, helping in the defense of the tower of the Petit Pont, and who escaped by virtue of swimming across the Seine to find safety on the Île-de-la-Cité.

[94] At this stage, we need to supplement what Abbo tells us with another source, the *Chronicon* of Regino of Prüm, where we learn that when the Vikings abandoned the siege of 885, they portaged overland, and again floated their vessels just past the Île-de-Saint-Louis, from where they made their way down into the Loire valley. See Carroll Gillmor, "War on the Rivers: Viking Numbers and Mobility on the Seine and Loire, 841–886," *Viator* 19 (1988): 79–109, esp. 88–9.

[95] Ebolus's trek is a bit of a distance, since the Vikings were camped around the area of the church and abbey of Saint-Germain-des-Prés—which is why Abbo observes that the abbot ran all the way there and back.

[96] These Danes are those still in the camp, which Ebolus thought was empty. Here we see Abbo's admiration for the tenacity with which the Vikings fight.

[97] By giving voice to the land of Neustria, his native region, Abbo presents a framed story in Book I, which began with Lutetia, or Paris, speaking and asking Abbo to compose a poem about the Viking attack. This structure serves to present a panoramic view of the Danish incursions: whereas Book I began with a particular city, it ends with a broader region, both of which undergo similar suffering. Perhaps there is also a subtler subtext here—why would God allow a Christian land to be ravaged by pagans? The answer will come at the end of Book II, and in the entirety of Book III.

[98] This is a telling observation, since it highlights the essential otherness of the Vikings—they are utterly blind to the nature of holy places in civilized society. For them, a church is merely an enclosed place that makes for a good corral. Here we see a juxtaposition of wilderness and the city, and the two cannot achieve any sort of harmony. When the animals are herded into the church, they perish—just as the Danes, who died earlier when they sought to storm the church. The two are of the same nature, Abbo is cleverly emphasizing. In short, neither civilization nor wilderness can contain the other without destroying or altering it.

[99] Abbo gives an interesting interpretation of why the herded animals died and their flesh rotted: Saint Germain took them as an offering and therefore they were rendered useless to the pagan Danes.

[100] Godfried was the count of Maine and defender of Chartres. The Oddo mentioned here is not to be confused with Odo, count of Paris. This Oddo is perhaps the brother of Rotbert the Quiver, and the Lord of Dunois and Chartrain. In order to differentiate the two Odos, Abbo tells us that Oddo had a prosthetic hand made of iron. As for Count Uddo, he might be the Utto mentioned in line 245 earlier; nothing further is known about him.

[101] Chartres had been captured earlier in 858 by the Viking chieftain Hasting or Hastein, whose exploits are recounted in Wace's *The Roman de Rou*, trans. Glyn S. Burgess (Jersey: Société Jersiaise, 2002); see Part II, lines 5, 13, 14, 412, 472, 473, 480, 488, 492, 499, 502.

[102] The account in Book II begins in March of 886. By mentioning that Paris is being defended by Bishop Gozlin (there is no mention of Count Odo, which is telling), Abbo guides us to consider that the ultimate salvation of Paris will come not from earthly lords, but from the heavenly one—and just as Paris will be saved by God, so too will a person's soul. As for Heinrich the Saxon, he was the count of Fulda, and had been appointed by Charles the Fat as commander in charge of resisting the Vikings, whom he had driven back from Saxony and the area of the Rhine valley in 885.

[103] "Far too few" suggests that Heinrich was not very successful in his onslaughts, despite Abbo's praise of him. It is important to note that Abbo does not have great faith or trust in mortal rulers, for they are either weak, promote self-interest, or are ineffective. This sets up the need for divine intercession.

[104] The Vikings also seem to behave differently from the Franks; they are especially prone to loud shrieks and shouts—something, curiously enough, the Franks do not indulge in. Perhaps this highlights again the savage nature of the Danes and their unchristian character. Their actions and behavior are forever outside the pale of Frankish decorum.

105 This second attack came at the beginning of March, 886.

106 These three gnomic lines constitute Abbo's personal ruminations on the Viking assaults. The tradition of such verse is strong in Germanic literature, as exampled in Old English. See *Anglo-Saxon Poetry*, ed. and trans. S. A. J. Bradley (London/Melbourne/Toronto: Dent, 1982), 344–50, 512–5.

107 In Germanic heroic tradition, it was the duty of retainers to stand by their lord in battle, and if he fell, to die with him. This is observed as early as Tacitus, who coined the phrase *comitatus*, with which he described the special bond that existed between a Germanic lord and his retainers. See *The Germania*, chaps. 12 and 14. Cf. the Anglo-Saxon term *gedryht*.

108 That is, Heinrich went back to Saxony, his own land, at the end of March or the beginning of April, having failed to rout the Vikings.

109 The Oratory of Saint-Germain-le-Rond, where now the Church of Saint-Germain-l'Auxerrois stands on the North shore of the Seine, was built in the sixth century. During this second attack the Vikings destroyed it.

110 That is, Saint-Germain-des-Prés.

111 It is likely that the Vikings made the church of Saint-Germain-des-Prés into a fortress, as evidenced by the building of ramparts. Abbo sees this desecration as accruing shame on the Franks. The Saint allows this in order to punish the Franks for their many sins, which is a theme that Abbo will soon begin to emphasize.

112 It appears that Siegfried is personally paid this ransom of sixty silver pounds by the Abbey of Saint-Germain-des-Prés—and not by the city of Paris.

113 This rather extended conceit imagines the Seine as some waterfowl being swallowed whole by the monstrous waters of the Channel, much as a cormorant might swallow a fish. We should not see this metaphor as mere embellishment, for it has a subtext—a wish that King Siegfried and his Vikings might sail up the Seine and be swallowed up and destroyed by the waters of the Channel, never to be seen again.

114 This ironic speech also suggests that Siegfried is certainly no king as Abbo and the Franks understand the office, since his men will do as they wish.

115 That is, the Île-de-la-Cité. This line offers further confirmation that the abbey, and not Paris, paid the ransom to Siegfried.

116 The conceit of the sea-monster-Channel is here brought to conclusion by inversion, in that the Seine now swallows the Vikings.

117 This is an interesting statement, since it implies settlement rather than a mere marauding expedition. By the time of the *Bella*, Vikings had begun to settle in the areas they overran, rather than merely ravaging them and sailing back to their home bases outside of France.

118 Perhaps there was a further offer of ransom; or more likely Abbo implies that they did not wish to take a smaller portion of the protection money from Siegfried.

119 Bishop Gozlin died on April 16, 886.

120 Hugo is called both "abbot" and "prince" because he was not only a clergyman but also the marquis of Neustria, a title he succeeded to after the death of Robert the Strong (the father of Count Odo). Hugo died on May 12, 886, likely a victim of the plague that struck the besieged city.

121 Abbo is mistaken about the death of Eberhard, the archbishop of Sens, who died the following year on February 1, 887.

122 This reaction of the Vikings is informed by the complaint of the Psalmist in Psalm 2. In fact, the appearance of Germain at this point suggests an acute awareness of this scriptural context, which speaks of the heathen being destroyed and the righteous prevailing.

123 The entombed mortal remains of a saint were thought to emit a sweet odor, according to the doctrine of incorruptibility, which was strongly adhered to during Abbo's time and indeed later, and which maintained that the bodies of saints did not decay. The perfume that emitted from the tomb was a sign both of God's favor and of the saint's efficacy.

[124] The cruelty of the Danes extends not only to the Franks but even to their beasts of burden, as well as their land, which is being trampled, ravaged, and burned. The suffering brought by the Vikings afflicts all things "Frankish"— the country, the people, the city.

[125] The miracle in this instance is the stalled cart, which has been laden with plundered grain, and which does not move despite the great number of oxen the Vikings have hitched to pull it free of the mud.

[126] It seems the Vikings simply took away the grain that was loaded on to the cart. Miracle aside, Abbo suggests that the amount of the looted grain was so great that no number of oxen could pull it.

[127] This incident should be read within the context of Psalm 7:15–16, for Abbo sees this "strange" death as part of the divine plan, which will ultimately lead to the salvation of Paris.

[128] It is likely that the man who suffered the consequences of this strange miracle was a Dane, for his soul goes down into Hell. On the other hand, he might also be a Frank who is punished for his willful disregard of a holy prohibition. Once again, Germain is protecting his earthly possessions.

[129] Marcellus, or Saint Marcel, was the bishop of Paris from 417 to 436, and Clodoald, or Saint Cloud, who died ca. 560, was the grandson of Clovis, and who was the very first king of the Franks.

[130] This dream vision of the sick nobleman points to the wonder-working miracles of Germain, who transforms weakness and fear into courage and strength. As well, we are now fully transported into the realm of magical realism.

[131] Germain has now taken charge of the defense of his city, a task in which the earthly rulers have entirely failed. The Vikings are likened to ravening wolves.

[132] The power of Germain resides in two acts, the spoken word and the miraculous deed—a contrast with the power of the rulers, which relies on two entirely different acts: ransom and expediency.

[133] Odo likely left in the latter part of May, 886, and he probably went to seek help from other lords, rather than from Charles the Fat, who was in Italy at this time.

[134] This is Abbot Ebolus.

[135] These guerilla, or hit-and-run, tactics are time-buying measures, while the Parisians wait for Odo's return. The siege of the Vikings has sealed off the city entirely.

[136] That is, the Île-de-la-Cité.

[137] The attack is concentrated along the Northwestern sector of the Île-de-la-Cité, where the fortifications had many gaps and the walls were quite low.

[138] Nothing further is known about the twins Segebert and Segevert, but compare the latter's name with the Old English one, Sigeferth.

[139] The original reads *cacumina Martis*, or "hill of Mars." In fact, the name "Montmartre" stems not from *mons martyrum*, "hill of the martyrs," but from *mons Mercoris*, "Hill of Mercury." It is likely that Odo returned from his mission, with fresh troops, at the end of June 886.

[140] That is, the rays of the sun (Helios) catch the battalions of Odo, which are ranged upon the heights of Montmartre, before falling upon the meadows and fields below.

[141] A league, or a *leuca* or *leuga* (a Celtic borrowing into Latin), was one Gallic mile, or about 1,500 Roman paces, which equals a little over 2 kilometers.

[142] This is the same Adalhelm mentioned in Book I, line 452, who is the nephew of Rotbert the Quiver.

[143] Count Heinrich died on August 28, 886. He was buried in the Abbey of Saint-Médard in Soissons, which now exists as a rather sad ruin on the outskirts of Soissons. Nothing but the remnant of the crypt remains.

[144] There is another Sinric, who in 887 laid siege to Sens, but failed to capture it. Abbo does tell us that Charles the Fat paid ransom and also allowed the Vikings to proceed to Sens; see Book II, lines 338, 420, and 429. Perhaps the famous Rollo, the first duke of Normandy, was allied with Sinric.

[145] The irony of Sinric's demise according to his boast allows Abbo to glimpse once more the workings of the divine will in human affairs.

[146] Again, Abbo anthropomorphizes in order to stress that the struggle is one undertaken not only by the inhabitants of Paris, but by every animate and inmate thing which inhabits the Christian world.

[147] That is, the conflict has grown and become more intense.

[148] The "front" end of Paris would be its Eastern part. Sainte-Geneviève (419 or 422–512) is the first patron saint of Paris. She was inspired to take holy orders by Saint Germain, whom she had met when she was a child; she lived most of her life in Paris. It is said that in 451 she saved the city from the marauding Huns, led by Attila. Upon her death, her body was buried in the Church of Mont-lès-Paris, which was renamed in her honor. During times of distress, Parisians often bore the relics of their saint around the city as they prayed for her intercession, a custom that Abbo mentions.

[149] As is the case with many of the bold warriors, whose deeds Abbo describes and thereby remembers, Gerbold is otherwise unknown. But perhaps the very fact that we still read of their courageous deeds is testimony enough.

[150] Again, it is worth noting that Abbo clearly sees the fight as a struggle between good and evil, between the righteous, Christian Franks and the godless, pagan Vikings.

[151] This dramatic scene certainly demonstrates ritualized lamentation and mourning. There has been no study of the association of women with the public expression of grief in Germanic society.

[152] That is, Saint Germain, rather than Count Odo.

[153] Thetis was a sea nymph in classical myth, and the mother of the hero Achilles. She was often referred to as being "born of the brine."

[154] Portunus was the Roman god of ports and harbors, which is why Abbo uses him to represent water.

[155] The Basilica of Saint Stephen Martyr (no longer extant) stood a little to the West of Notre Dame Cathedral. The saint referred to is Germain, not Stephen.

[156] An elegant encapsulation of the salvific process, which the entire *Bella* consistently foregrounds—that is, the passage from a state of sin into the state of grace.

[157] That is, the Church of Saint-Germain-des-Prés.

[158] There were three churches along this part of the wall: Saint-Merry, Saint-Jacques, and Saint-Leufroy; none of these is extant today.

[159] Nothing further is known about these two brothers.

[160] King Charles the Fat was in Paris by October 24, 886.

[161] Anscheric was the abbot of Saint-Germain-d'Auxerre; he died in 910.

[162] The abruptness of this passage is curious; perhaps there is an implicit critique of Charles the Fat's behavior: instead of fighting the Danes, he chooses to pay them off, and then allows them quick passage into Burgundy, where they are free to carry on pillaging.

[163] Charles the Fat died on January 13, 888, in Neidingen.

[164] This reads like a barb aimed at Burgundy, which did not send troops to aid Paris during the siege. The reference to marriage likely implies that some of the Danes settled down and married Neustrian women, as evidenced by what occurred about some thirty years onwards with the creation of the Duchy of Normandy, the French Danelaw, an area that Abbo knew as Neustria, his home. It has also been suggested that this remark refers to the marriage of Count Odo with a daughter of Audran, the Count of Troyes.

[165] Under Sinric (perhaps the same one mentioned by Abbo earlier), the Vikings besieged Sens on November 30, 886. But they had little success. They returned to Paris at the end of May 887.

[166] The miracles that follow come immediately after the arrival again of the Vikings and their requisitioning of the church of Saint-Germain-des-Prés. This should be read as a controlled juxtaposition of the impending threat posed by the marauders and its ultimate neutralization by Saint Germain, whose power to undertake such a defense is highlighted by these miracles. Moreover, these healings point to the notion that the Saint is a far worthier protector of Paris than either King Charles the Fat or Count Odo. Thus, he is the true hero of the poem.

[167] This well was likely located near the chancel of Saint-Germain-des-Prés, where a cloister was also once located.

[168] There is an implicit critique of this priest who chooses to sell the curative water for a good profit. This is one of the first indications by Abbo of internal corruption, which has led to God's wrath, which in turn has brought the Vikings as a scourge for the many sins of the Franks.

[169] Water turning into blood, of course, harks back to the first of the ten plagues in Egypt (Exodus 7:19). Abbo is suggesting that this occurrence is not only a punishment for the blasphemy of the pagan women, but it is also a warning to the Franks, who like the Egyptians neither hear nor obey God's commandments.

[170] Virgil's *Aeneid* (Book VI, lines 625–6) is the source for this expression. As an interesting parallel, the same turn of phrase is also found in the Second Sermon of Saint John of Damascus (ca. 675–749).

[171] That is, Germain, Abbo's spiritual father.

[172] It is said that Germain's mother was prevented from aborting him by a revelation from God that her son would be a saint.

[173] According to legend, John the Baptist also brought back to life three dead men.

[174] Here, Abbo makes explicit his point that the princes (King Charles, Count Odo, and Count Heinrich) have all failed Paris, whereas Saint Germain has not.

[175] This song of the people of Paris, or by the city itself, clearly presents Germain as a wondrous defender, and therefore the hero of the entire poem.

[176] Philomela is a nightingale. The name derives from a Greek myth. Philomela was a daughter of King Pandion of Athens, and the sister of Procne, whose husband, Tereus, raped her; to keep Philomela silent, he cut out her tongue. But Philomela told her woeful tale by weaving it into a tapestry. To avenge the crime, Procne, Medea-like, killed her own son, cooked him, and fed him to Tereus. When he learned the awful deed he had done, he sought to kill both the sisters. But the gods changed all of them into birds. Tereus became a hoopoe, Procne a swallow, and Philomela a nightingale, which sings its plaintiff song when the sun sets.

[177] Since the Vikings are pagan, Abbo sees them as little better than animals; hence they live in caves. Also, this observation highlights their otherness.

[178] Because of their essential falseness, since they are godless, the Vikings easily break oaths. In Frankish, and Germanic, society oaths were a fundamental principle of civilized life. Since the Vikings are heathens, they are uncivilized, and therefore are inveterate oath-breakers—a crime Abbo and his society would have considered most heinous. See Alexander C. Murray, *Germanic Kinship Structure* (Toronto: Pontifical Institute of Mediaeval Studies, 1983), 157–62. For comparison, also see *The Burgundian Code*, trans. Katherine Fischer Drew (Philadelphia: University of Pennsylvania Press, 1972), 52.

[179] The Vikings face the problem of not being able to sail down the Seine because of the two bridges, the Petit Pont and the Grand Pont. Their plan is to break through by ramming them. Perhaps Abbo is thinking of the Petit Pont alone, which was made of wood and could conceivably be rammed and broken apart. But the Grand Pont was made of stone and therefore impossible to ram. "Chariots of Thetis" refers to ships.

[180] That is, noon. Both Anscheric and Ebolus are manning the city; Odo is still absent.

[181] *Acephali* ("headless") is what Abbo calls the Vikings in the original. This is a crucial observation since it explains the actions of the Danes—their rapacity and their willingness to break oaths.

[182] *Solito securum*, says Abbo, "assurance," which was a guarantee given to back up an oath. Perhaps the Vikings gave hostages to assure the Franks of their "good behavior."

[183] Perhaps the cause of this marveling is the idea that Christians and pagans can indeed live together—as strange as humans cohabiting with animals, in Abbo's eyes. From another perspective, this shows the permanent quality of the Norse incursions: they are not interested so much in raids as in securing land, moveable wealth, and women.

[184] Perhaps this explains why the Vikings lifted the siege of Sens and did not sack it.

[185] Here is found a gloss in the manuscript that reads: *ENIGMA: carbo si feurit munitus flamma et cinere, semper vivit, alioquin moritur* ("A riddle: if a coal is protected by fire and ash, it lives always, otherwise it dies"). The meaning of this line has eluded most. However, we can recover its meaning if we read it as a simile for the Christian prisoners who have been left exposed among the pagans, and because they are no longer nourished and protected by their Christian community (the ash and the flame), they shall die, just like exposed coals. Ash makes for an excellent way to keep coals alive to start the next fire. It is also possible to read a subtle warning in this simile. Christians, when they become exposed to ungodly ways, shall die (perhaps Abbo has in mind those who have openly cohabited with the Vikings).

[186] Abbo has already foregrounded the breaking of this oath earlier when he called the Vikings "headless."

[187] It seems that these "fifty" are the hostages whom the Vikings gave as a guarantee for the "assurance" earlier.

[188] This line should properly be read as a criticism of Ebolus. More importantly, it ties in with Abbo's underlying theme—that men in power are flawed and therefore cannot carry out the duties given them. Since Ebolus serves not only a clerical role but also a political one, he is open to Abbo's wider critique of leaders and princes. In fact, thus far, priests tend not to be portrayed favorably, with the exception of Gozlin. We have already met the priest who sells the holy water from Germain's well, and now we the true nature of Ebolus, who is flawed by greed and lust.

[189] Again, the idea that only the hostages were killed is reinforced. Abbo seems also be to criticizing Anscheric for letting some of the captives go, who set out and besiege Meaux; this happened in the summer of 888.

[190] As noted earlier, Charles the Fat died on January 13, 888, a dejected man, for he saw part of his Eastern kingdom taken from him by his nephew Arnulf, to whom many of his own followers deserted. It is curious that Abbo uses classical, and therefore pagan, terminology to describe the passage of Charles's soul. Perhaps we can construe this as a subtle critique of God's revenge, since Charles was a poor pastor to the flock he had been given. In Roman mythology, Ops was a chthonic deity and was the wife of Saturn. She was the goddess of abundance, and therefore of the earth, from which all riches flow.

[191] Odo was crowned king at Compiègne on February 29, 888.

[192] Abbo differentiates between Neustria and France; the latter, in his day, referred to the territory North of the Seine only.

[193] Richard of Autun (ca. 867–921) was the duke of Burgundy; he was the first to hold this title.

[194] The three parts being the kingdoms of East Francia, Middle Francia, and West Francia.

[195] This expedition occurred in the spring of 889. Not long after Odo's coronation, Duke Ranulph II declared himself king of Aquitaine.

[196] Abbo's chronology is a little confused here, since the Vikings besieged Meaux from June to October of 888, while Odo marched against Aquitaine in 889.

[197] Count Tetbert, the brother of Bishop Anscheric, died at this siege, as we read later. Delos is the island where Apollo was born. Therefore, it means "the sun."

[198] A rather wry comment by Abbo, just after he tells us that no leader came to the aid of Meaux.

[199] Odo returned to Paris from Aquitaine in June of 889.

[200] Despite the gathering of a great host, Odo could not engage the Vikings, because of internal disagreements. Therefore, Odo, like Charles the Fat before him who led a similarly large army to Paris, and paid ransom, so that the Vikings left and headed for the Contentin and then on to Brittany.

[201] Ademar was Odo's cousin.

[202] Nothing is known about this warrior; he is mentioned again in line 482.

[203] This is a curious paraphrase of Matthew 26:51–52.

[204] That is, Count Robert the Strong, the father of King Odo.

[205] A warrior-clergyman was not a contradiction in terms, as noted earlier.

[206] Odo defeated the Vikings in the forest of Montfaucon in the Argonne region on June 24, 889.

[207] The hunting horn was a prized possession of the Germanic warrior, along with the sword. Cf. the Ripon Charter Horn, which likely dates from 886. See Paul Hardwick, *Discovering Horn* (Guildford: Lutterworth Press, 1981), 50–5. Also cf. Roland's horn, Oliphant.

[208] The axe was the preferred weapon of the Vikings. Its use is much evident in the Bayeux Tapestry and among the pre-Conquest English (cf. the Housecarls). See Johannes Bronsted, *The Vikings* (Harmondsworth: Penguin Books, 1976), 122.

[209] That is, "on that single day."

[210] Aquitaine revolted twice against Odo: the first time in 889, and then again in 892. Abbo makes reference to the second revolt, which was led by the Abbot Ebolus (who earlier had worked with Odo to defend Paris) and his brother Gosbert. Both were killed; Ebolus in 892.

[211] The claim of Charles the Simple, the Carolingian heir to the throne, was championed by many of the nobles who had elected Odo in the first place—and in 894, the claim was also supported by King Arnulf (Charles's uncle), to whom Odo had sworn allegiance.

[212] Proserpina is the goddess of the underworld. As with Charles the Fat earlier, it is significant that Abbo refers to a pagan goddess when describing the rebellious deeds of Ademar. Perhaps implicit in such a reference is the fact that Ademar is fighting against an anointed king and his own kinsman—acts inherently "pagan" in Abbo's eyes.

[213] This Rotbert (mentioned earlier in Book I, line 67) is the future King Robert I, who ruled France from 922 to 923, and from whom the Capetians descended.

[214] William, known as "the Pious," was the count of Auvergne and duke of Aquitaine. He is most famous for having founded the Benedictine Abbey of Cluny, in 909, which would soon become an important center of learning.

[215] Likely the River Creuse.

[216] Count Hugo, who supported Odo, was given the territories confiscated from William the Pious, which led to a bitter conflict between the two. During this time, Odo had problems of his own, since Charles the Simple had been crowned king. William killed Count Hugo in 893, as we shall read later (lines 560–1).

[217] William the Pious ruled over a vast swath of territories, namely, the Auvergne, Gothia (present-day Languedoc-Roussillon), Berry, Mâcon, Lyonnaid, and Limousin.

[218] That is, 900.

[219] A reference to the coronation of Charles the Simple in January of 893 at Reims. This led to a civil war that lasted about four years.

[220] Charles the Simple was born posthumously to Adelaide of Paris, the third wife of King Louis the Stammerer (846–879).

[221] By "Germania" Abbo means the Northern parts of Francia, which Charles seized. Odo did not hasten to defend his claim, but remained in Aquitaine until the summer of 893.

[222] This likely refers to the siege of Reims, which Odo undertook soon after his return in the summer of 893.

[223] That is, Odo forgave those who had rebelled against him and supported Charles.

[224] Swentibold (870–900) was the illegitimate son of the Emperor Arnulf, who had given him the kingdom of Lotharingia to rule. Swentibold wanted more and entered into various intrigues against his half-brother (and the legitimate son of Arnulf), Louis the Child, and against West Francia, where both Charles the Simple and Odo united in order to rout him. Ragenar the count of Hainault killed Swentibold in 900.

225 The Vikings returned in the summer of 896 and numbered some 400 men; they had been wintering in Choisy-au-Bac.

226 This harsh critique of Odo begins the movement towards understanding the causes for the suffering wrought by the Vikings. Chief among these is the neglect of the rulers, that is, those whose holy duty is to protect the land and the people. It is with the greatest indignation that Abbo states that Odo will not keep his own honor intact much longer, because ultimately he too is a traitor, having betrayed the people he rules. Hereafter, the poem takes on a homiletic tone in order to explain why affliction has come to the Franks.

227 These three sins are important because they are peculiar to a very specific sector of the Frankish population—the highborn men, among whom the rulers are be to be counted. These sins have not afflicted the common folk.

228 We should bear in mind that this critique of the clergy is also focused on the highborn, since they too came from the nobility. The three sins that Abbo excoriates are sexual lust (especially homosexuality), greed, and pride. All three are fully addressed in Book III. For him, these three sins have brought the Danes upon Francia as God's scourge.

229 Tyrian, or royal, purple was a precious dye of the ancient world made from mollusks.

230 Odo died on New Year's Day 898 at La Fère-sur-Oise. Abbo no longer finds in Odo anything to sing about or praise.

231 By the "Foe" Abbo means the Devil, of course. However, by using the same discourse as he did in describing the fight with the Viking foe, he is emphasizing the salvific process that he wishes to highlight: just as the inhabitants of Paris struggled against the Vikings to win their salvation, so also must an individual struggle in order to save his or her soul.

232 The admonishment is to flee sexual desire, which leads the cleric into the clutches of the Devil. Of the three sins that Abbo mentioned earlier (Book II, lines 658ff.), he begins Book III with lust, which he stresses is the chief sin afflicting Frankish society. The entire third book, of course, is gnomic in nature.

233 Abbo as a witness to the siege by the Vikings allegorizes his experience and translates it into a moral lesson.

234 "Lucid perception" depends on the final goal that everyone must strive for—the life hereafter.

235 The double cure is faith—first it allays sin and then it leads to Heaven.

236 Such is the whole armor of the priest. Cf. Ephesians 6:10–18. Just as the warriors who confronted and defeated the devilish Vikings with their earthly armor, so too a righteous priest can fight the Devil with his own armor: the Scriptures, the vestments, the chalice.

237 These blemishes of the eye are those that come from an idle mind. Abbo sees writing as a pious act, since it keeps the mind occupied and thus distant from the urge to sin, which indolence brings.

238 Just like those brave warriors who were assisted by Saint Germain and successfully defended Paris.

239 The "herds" of the pimps are prostitutes, and their "dross" the sin that is incurred by visiting them.

240 The ill use of a mantle lies in its use as a piece of adornment, which leads to lust. Although there is a strong misogynist streak in the third book, Abbo excoriates men even more.

241 And not suitable for witchcraft.

242 The "inheritor" is someone who is the heir to Heaven. Classical tradition knows two men by the name of Codrus. One was the last king of Athens, who sacrificed his own life, when the Dorians invaded, to save his kingdom. An oracle had proclaimed that if the king of Athens were killed, the Dorians would be defeated. They, therefore, took great care not to kill Codrus. But he thwarted their carefully laid intentions and contrived to have himself killed by a Dorian warrior. We should certainly read this as an ironic comment on the kings and rulers who hold sway over the Franks—whom Abbo specifically sees as having forgotten their rightful duty—to protect the people given in their charge by God. The second Codrus is a Roman stereotype of a poetaster, who annoys people with his bad verses. Abbo sees in "Codrus" the summation of the righteous person, someone who sacrifices himself for salvation (of the soul, or of Paris), like the Athenian king, and someone who is unlike the Roman poetaster.

243 Abbo uses the word *fisco, fiscus*, which means "bag," but more commonly "testicles." The other meaning for it is "wicker basket," which makes little sense in this context. Grabbing the testicles of an unruly horse subdues it, because of the threat of pain. Thus, given the obvious biological difference, Abbo suggests that a disobedient woman should be subdued by force. The apposition, however, is more than a little curious.

244 That is, let your speech be made sweet with wisdom.

245 The task of the medieval geographer was not to record the physical description of the earth, but to further the salvific process—to show the workings of God to save humankind. See Natalia Lozovsky, *The Earth Is Our Book: Geographical Knowledge in the Latin West, ca. 400–1000* (Ann Arbor: University of Michigan Press, 2000).

246 The admonition here is against homosexuality. By "geldings" Abbo implies fellow monks who have dedicated themselves to complete celibacy.

247 That is, do not become an idle chatterer and gossipmonger.

248 Just like the warriors who defended Paris, with the help of Saint Germain.

249 The dais is the place where a teacher stands and lectures.

250 That is, heaven.

251 That is, pay attention to the details.

252 Humility leads to piety, which leads to love, which destroys hatred.

253 That is, do not covet the wealth of others.

254 Abbo is purposely being crude, as in line 43 above, in order to stress the vileness of sin. Perhaps he has in mind the word used by Saint Paul in his letter to the Philippians 3:8 (*skubala*), which has the same meaning.

255 The "forest-levy" is *lucar*, which was a tax put on forests to support actors. But here, the "forest-levy's wealth" simply means fruit.

256 Piety should adorn the pious and not jewelry (which brings out vanity). However, Abbo does allow kings their finery.

257 This fourfold path to salvation counters the assault of the three sins Abbo has already highlighted. By "praise," the praise of God is meant—and not self-praise.

258 The "life of discipline" is centered on the fourfold path. Dying of "heart-strain" points to excess.

259 That is, there is greater strength in smaller things, than in bigger, more ostentatious ones.

260 A heart suffers when it is restrained and not allowed to indulge its desires.

261 According to medieval bestiaries, goats were perceived as extremely lascivious and always eager to copulate, because, it was said, their blood was extremely hot. Abbo is saying that the path of lust leads nowhere.

262 Just as the Vikings plundered the riches of Francia and Burgundy.

263 The "native city" is heaven, the City of God.

264 The image is that of a careful gardener who has wisely pruned and has eradicated the blight of sin, in order to reap a rich harvest.

265 Bacchus, the god of wine, that is drunkenness, taints the good wine of a pious life with the worm of lust.

266 The "darkest field" is where sin is rank.

267 Abbo apposes the eunuch (an incomplete man) with a man entire. By doing so, he suggests that sin emasculates. The man completed by faith is sorrowful because he knows that true joy can never be experienced in this world, but only in the hereafter. Instead of losing himself in a bright palace like a eunuch, he prepares for the hereafter—by thinking about the grave.

268 Virtue should remain hidden, because if it becomes manifest it can lead to pride.

269 Just as Saint Germain remained with the Parisians and protected them from the Satanic Vikings.

General Index

Index of Modern Authors

PRINTED ON PERMANENT PAPER • IMPRIME SUR PAPIER PERMANENT • GEDRUKT OP DUURZAAM PAPIER - ISO 9706

N.V. PEETERS S.A., WAROTSTRAAT 50, B-3020 HERENT